LOCAL GOVERNMENT
in
SCOTLAND

LOCAL GOVERNMENT
in
SCOTLAND

SECOND EDITION

By

GEORGE MONIES
Former member, City of Edinburgh District Council

and

GARRY COUTTS
Member, City of Edinburgh District Council

EDINBURGH
W. GREEN & SON LTD.
Law Publishers
St. Giles Street
1989

First published in 1985
Second edition 1989

ISBN 0   414   00889   8

Cover photograph of Strathclyde Region Headquarters
courtesy of Strathclyde Regional Council

Printed in Great Britain by the Eastern Press Ltd

PREFACE

THE first edition of this book referred to the difficulty of writing about local government at a time of change. Some changes were anticipated but few could have foreseen the pace of change in local government in the last four years. The Conservative government, returned in the election of 1987, has continued its previous policies of radical alteration to the powers of local authorities. Although the structure of local government in Scotland has not altered, the powers and functions have. In addition there will be restructuring of the financing of local services in the next few years. Hence the reason for this second edition.

Some critics of the first edition were concerned about the compactness of the text but the author and publishers were aiming to get a balance between length and price given that the purpose of the book was to reach students and interested onlookers. It made no pretence to be a technical or academic study of local government. This second edition has the same purpose.

As with the first edition the authors would like to thank friends, councillors and officials who have contributed their advice and knowledge, with a special thanks to officials of the City of Edinburgh District Council. Some cynics will no doubt comment that since the powers of local government have been reduced considerably in the last few years there will be no need for a third edition.

George Monies would like to dedicate this book to his children, Helen and Paul, to his mother, and to the memory of his father, James Monies. Garry Coutts would like to dedicate the book to his wife, Liz, who not only typed drafts but looked after their children while he wrote, read drafts and corrected proofs, and to Yla and Angus who did not ask "who are you?".

Edinburgh   G.M.
March 1989   G.C.

CONTENTS

CHAPTER 1

HISTORICAL DEVELOPMENT

LOCAL government has a long history in Scotland but it was only in the nineteenth century that a structure was developed. Inevitably the structure had to be changed to meet changing circumstances. The first major rationalisation of local government was in the 1890s; some minor changes were made after the First World War but it was felt necessary to restructure the system in the mid-1920s. The Local Government (Scotland) Act 1929 was the first comprehensive local government Act in Scotland but the changes made then proved not to be sufficient to cope with the large-scale problems after 1945.

Major changes in central government policies in the 1940s and 1950s brought criticism about the local government system and many local authorities found it difficult to carry out their statutory duties. The need for reform was recognised by the 1960s but opinion was divided on what structural changes were required to take the local government system into the last quarter of the twentieth century. It was for this reason that Royal Commissions were set up in 1966 and the Wheatley Report of 1969 proposed a radical reorganisation of local government in Scotland.

Most of the recommendations of the Wheatley Report were enacted in the Local Government (Scotland) Act 1973 and subsequent legislation. Successive governments since then have attempted to tidy up the system. The Conservative governments elected since 1979 have, however, redefined the role of local authorities. This redefinition has led to a variety of legislation affecting the powers, functions and management of local government in Scotland although not, so far, to the extent of abolition of certain local authorites—a fate which befell some local authorities in England.

The Burgh System

The core which ran through local government and local administration in Scotland until 1975 was the burgh. The first burghs were established by David I in the first half of the twelfth century. The purpose of the burgh was twofold. In the absence of any effective method of controlling the country, i.e. a legal system and an army, the Crown established garrisons in strategic positions. In return for protection the burgh was given a monopoly of foreign and local trade. The Crown extracted revenue from this granting of monopoly, some of which was used for the upkeep of the garrison. Therefore law and order and trade were the initial responsibilities of the burghs.

There was however, at the same time, the development of "free burghs". These were established by nobles and bishops on their own land. Free burghs were granted local trading privileges by the Crown. Glasgow is a good example of a free burgh established by a bishop. These burghs were sometimes called "burghs of barony" or "burghs of regality".

As trade grew in the sixteenth and seventeenth centuries so did the number of burghs. By the beginning of the eighteenth century over 300 burghs had been established—some however did not survive. Each burgh was a compact community, close-knit and well regulated. Many of them had clearly defined boundaries or "marches", and "tolbooths" where traders paid dues to enter the burgh market.

The royal burghs were very powerful and generally governed by a self-electing council. The local landowner had a considerable say in the composition and decisions of the council. The royal burghs also sent representatives to the Scots Parliament. The non-royal burghs varied in composition and power but few were as independent as royal burghs. Some attempted to break into the trading monopoly of the royal burghs.

Apart from the burghs, local affairs like education and poor relief were the responsibility of kirk sessions after 1560. The cost of education and poor relief was met by the heritors or landowners in each parish. Some of the wealthier landowners were nominated by the Crown "commissioners of supply" which meant that they were responsible for collecting revenues. Each county also had "justices of the peace" who were responsible for public order and the maintenance of the highways.

With the growth of industry in the nineteenth century came the growth of population. This growth was concentrated around particular centres in west central Scotland. The result was that local services like sanitation, water, education, etc., came under strain. In addition towns expanded outside the old burgh boundaries.

In order to cope with these problems, Parliament created a number of new authorities. After 1845 poor relief was transferred from the kirk sessions to elected parochial boards. Public health became the responsibility of parochial boards and burgh councils. The powers of town councils and burgh commissioners were extended to cover police, punishment of offenders and some

sanitary matters. Finally, by 1872 education became the responsibility of elected school boards—one for each parish.

During this period reforms were made to the burgh system. The
old self-elected councils were swept away and a measure of popular
election to town councils was established. In addition many of the
new town councils were given powers to raise money for their
services by rating.

In landward areas, the powers of the commissioners of supply
were extended. In addition to law and order and roads they were
given control of the militia, authority for levying rates, control of
police, registration of electors and appointment of valuation
assessors.

From 1889 to 1894 local government was reformed. Commissioners and boards of supply had many of their powers taken over
by elected county councils. By 1894 elected parish councils (in
landward areas and in burghs) had taken over a variety of local
affairs including some of the responsibilities of the parochial
boards. By the end of the century Scottish local government
consisted of:

County councils	33
Burgh councils	200
Parish councils	869

Numerous other authorities included burgh police commissioners,
county road boards, county district committees, burgh and parochial school boards.

In 1918 there was further rationalisation of local government.
About 1,000 school boards were replaced by directly elected
education authorities numbering 38. These were often referred to
as ad hoc education authorities.

In 1929, a major reform of local government took place. The
Local Government (Scotland) Act 1929 abolished parish councils,
district committees, standing joint committees and the old royal,
parliamentary and police burghs. These burghs were replaced
by a twofold classification of burghs—large burghs (having a
population over 20,000) and small burghs (having a population over
2,000). County councils and counties of cities (a new classification)
became education authorities replacing the ad hoc education
authorities. In the landward areas of counties certain local services
became the responsibility of district councils. The 1929 system
therefore consisted of:

Counties of cities (all-purpose)	4
County councils	33
Large burghs	21
Small burghs	176
District councils	196

Apart from the four cities the 1929 system could be described as a four-tier system.

Post-War Problems

The reorganisation of 1929 was no doubt intended to last for many years, but no one could have predicted the events of the next 20 years. The 1930s saw massive unemployment which created strains on the social services, many of them still the responsibility of local authorities. Indeed some local authorities in England were forced to declare themselves bankrupt. The Second World War again altered the role of local authorities. The central government had extensive economic, financial and social powers and the local authorities became agents of central administration.

By 1945, therefore, the 1929 system had hardly had a chance to function under normal circumstances. In the period after 1945, the basis of the welfare state was laid. The post-war Labour government decided that in running certain basic services many local authorities were too small. It transferred some hitherto local government functions to administrative (non-elected) agencies and government departments. These services included hospitals, national assistance, electricity and gas.

At the same time the central government expanded the social services and many of the larger local authorities were given statutory powers in these areas, e.g. education, child welfare, etc. Certain other powers were given to local authorities. These had been nationally run during the war and included the police, the fire service and land-use planning.

The result of these post-war changes meant that the 1929 structure had put upon it a whole range of new powers and services which it was not designed to take. In addition the scale of many local authority functions had changed. The Wheatley report instanced the police service. In 1862 a population of 700 was felt to be adequate to support a separate police force; in 1899 a minimum population of 7,000 was laid down; in 1929 no small burgh (population less than 20,000) was allowed to have a police force; the Scottish Home and Health Department now think in terms of a minimum population of 250,000 for a police authority.

With changes in the range, nature and scale of local authority functions after 1945 there also came increased central government control of local authority decision-making. The trend in central government administration since 1945 has been towards greater economic and social planning. These administrative controls through general Acts like the Local Government (Scotland) Act 1947 and specific Acts like the Education Act have required local authorities to conform to certain minimum standards laid down by central government and also to seek approval from the Secretary of State for Scotland for a host of other actions.

To statutory and administrative controls have been added financial controls. The Treasury, in their evidence to the Wheatley Commission, put it this way:

> "local authorities have become, over an ever-increasing part of their activities, the instruments for carrying out social policies whose broad framework is determined nationally by the Departments concerned and by the Government collectively. It is therefore inescapable that the central government, and in particular the Treasury, should be increasingly concerned with the need for forward planning and effective control of the movement of local authority expenditure as a whole."

This brief description of the development of local government in Scotland brings out two main features. First, with the growth of local services the small local authority found it increasingly difficult to survive. Thus we saw, with each reform, the disappearance of parish councils, school boards and eventually, in the 1970s, the small and large burghs.

Secondly, the ever-increasing involvement of central government, particularly in the fields of economic and social planning, meant that local authorities were dealing more and more with central government and often under the close supervision of central government departments.

The general direction of local government, therefore, was always to larger units, and central government was a party to encouraging this, because it felt that larger units would mean more efficient local government. However, as many were to argue, larger units meant less democratic local government. It was this problem which the Wheatley Commission attempted to solve between 1966 and 1969.

The Wheatley Report
The Royal Commission on Local Government in Scotland was set up in May 1966 under the chairmanship of Lord Wheatley.

The commission had, including the chairman, nine members of whom three were MPs. The remit of the commission was as follows:

"To consider the structure of local government in Scotland in relation to its existing functions; and to make recommendations for authorities and boundaries, and for functions and their divisions, having regard to the size and character of areas in which these can be most effectively exercised and the need to sustain a viable system of local democracy."

The commission interpreted its terms of reference as excluding consideration of administrative or legislative devolution and new methods of finance for local government. The commission, however, felt that it could consider the transfer of functions from government or other agencies to local government and that there was no specific limit to its consideration of the size or scale of local government units. The commission's approach was to analyse the then existing local government system and to lay down certain basic objectives for a reformed or re-organised system.

The commission's report, published in 1969, sets out the basic factors to be considered when devising a new structure:

- Local government exists to provide services or exercise *functions*.
- The functions have to be exercised over suitable *areas*.
- The functions and areas have to be brought together to form *authorities*.

The commission felt that a strong case had been made out for certain services to be provided over very wide areas—planning, personal social services, housing, police and fire, roads, water and industrial development.

The Royal Commission's general approach to local government was not to tinker with the existing system but to scrap it altogether and start from scratch. Many of the views about size and efficiency were accepted and thus the idea of large regional authorities was proposed. The new district authorities were given a very minor role to play. This emphasis on regionalism reflected the ideas of the day. Central government had, administratively, regionalised many of its own departments and the newer concept of economic planning was based on regional economies.

In restructuring local government a general philosophy or approach was required to justify the radical changes. Thus the commission developed the ideas of power, effectiveness, local democracy and local involvement. These ideas, however, have been reduced to the single idea of trying to reconcile bigger local government units with "grass roots" democracy. Many commentators argued that the report failed to reconcile these two concepts, and that the recommendations emphasised big units at the expense of democracy.

The 1973 Act and after

Although the Wheatley report had been largely accepted by a Labour government, it fell to the subsequent Conservative government to enact the proposals. A White Paper, *Reform of Local Government in Scotland*, was issued in 1971. That White Paper reflected the views of Conservatives in Scotland. There was a change of emphasis away from the regional predominance of the Wheatley Report to a more evenly divided two-tier system. The 1971 White Paper added one more region—the Borders—and took Argyll from the Highland Region and added it to Strathclyde. Orkney and Shetland became "most-purpose" authorities and the number of districts was increased from 37 to 49 with housing becoming a district function.

Before the publication of the Bill the government announced more changes to the White Paper. The Western Isles were extracted from the Highland Region and given "most purpose" responsibilities like Orkney and Shetland. The result of this was to reduce the number of districts from 49 to 47.

During the passage of the Local Government (Scotland) Bill further changes were made due to considerable public pressure and intriguing cross-party alliances in Parliament. The final result of these changes was to produce a structure of nine regional councils, 53 district councils and three islands councils.

The Local Government (Scotland) Act 1973 remains as the basic legislation of the reformed local government system in Scotland although there has been considerable dissatisfaction with it and many changes have been proposed and many implemented. Even before the new local authorities came into being in 1975 there were last minute legal attempts to halt them. After 1975, with a Labour government back in power, it was felt that the new system should be given a chance to settle down. Once again, however, with another change of government in 1979 dissatisfaction came to the surface.

Many Conservatives felt that there was wasteful duplication and overlapping in the functions of local authorities and the government therefore decided to set up, in 1980, a committee of inquiry to look at the concurrent functions of regional and district authorities.

The chairman of this committee was Mr A. Stodart, a former Conservative MP and Minister of State at the Scottish Office. The remit of the Stodart committee was essentially "to review the working relationship among authorities since 15 May 1975" and also "to recommend whether any transfer or rationalisation of functions between them is desirable and consistent with fully maintaining the viability of the existing authorities".

The committee reported in 1981 and its main proposals did not suggest any major alteration of the structure of local government. The main aim of the report was to "tidy up" overlapping areas between regions and districts. The committee rejected all- or most-purpose authorities and also rejected the argument about creating most-purpose status for the four city districts.

The main changes recommended by the committee were to (1) allow regional authorities sole rights to industrial development; (2) transfer the recreation and leisure functions of regional councils to the districts; (3) transfer community centres from regional councils to districts; (4) transfer all tourist responsibilities from regions to districts. There were other minor amendments to functions.

The government did not accept all the proposals of the Stodart report. Nevertheless the Local Government and Planning (Scotland) Act 1982 does, amongst other things, give effect to the major recommendations of the report. The Act reallocates functions between regions and districts. In industrial development the government decided, against the views of the Stodart committee, to allow industrial *promotion* to be the responsibility of regional councils while not changing the powers of any local authority to engage in industrial *development*.

Recreation and leisure functions, since 1983, have been the sole responsibility of district (and islands) authorities, as are countryside matters, nature conservation and tourism, although regions still have some minor responsibilities in these matters. In addition district councils were given sole powers to assist community councils. Others changes to the 1973 Act relate to rating and planning and are dealt with under these respective headings later.

CHAPTER 2

LOCAL AUTHORITY FUNCTIONS

THE following description of local authority functions is not intended to be exhaustive—that would need a complete book on its own. It is, however, intended to give a broad picture of the main functions. Some functions are exercised concurrently, e.g. planning, and it is, therefore, not easy to compartmentalise but a broad distinction is made between the responsibilities of the respective authorities. It was felt, in this edition, wiser to put the functions and structure of the Convention of Scottish Local Authorities in this chapter as the activities of that organisation are basically concerned with the various functions of local authorities.

Regional Functions
Education
Both in terms of people involved and money expended, education is the biggest single service provided by local authorities in Scotland. It would be easy to assume that education is mainly concerned with children, but education authorities provide a wide range of educational services for all ages. Perhaps the easiest division of education is into compulsory and non-compulsory.

Compulsory education in Scotland takes place between the ages of five and 16 years. Local authorities are obliged by statute to provide a place at an educational establishment for all children in their areas who are of school age. In addition to this the education authority is obliged to satisfy itself that school-age children who do not attend local authority schools are attending a recognised school or are receiving "adequate tuition".

In return for providing education for school-age children the local authority receives a grant (through the revenue support grant) from central government. Since education accounts for 45 per cent of the revenue support grant, naturally the Secretary of State, through the Scottish Education Department, has taken considerable supervisory powers over this service. Most of these powers are concerned with the laying down of standards and cover such items as qualifications of staff, class sizes, school organisation, standards of accommodation, school terms, school closures, catchment areas, etc.

Until recently local education authorities had the discretion to draw up school catchment areas. This meant that all school-age children in a particular area attended the designated school for that area. Some exceptions were made by the education committee for individual cases, e.g. partially handicapped children. These catchment areas were often drawn so as to achieve a satisfactory "social mix". However since 1981 there has existed the "parents' charter".

This legislation allows parents to send their children to the school of their choice. Local authorities can still draw up catchment areas but parents are not obliged to send their children to the designated school. The consequence of this development has been that, in many urban areas, there are now "popular" and "unpopular" schools. Paradoxically many of the "popular" schools have high rolls and large class sizes and "unpopular" schools have falling rolls and small class sizes. Because this latter type of school, often in low income areas, becomes less viable and, particularly at secondary level, restricts the subject choice of pupils, it is these schools which get threatened with closure.

As another example of the powers of the Secretary of State over aspects of educational provision there has been recent controversy about school closures. Because of falling school rolls central government has, for some time, been using its powers of persuasion to have local authorities rationalise schools systems by closing down schools with small and falling rolls. This was often a painful decision for local education committees who were usually pressurised by the local parents' and teachers' organisations to keep local schools open. Strathclyde Regional Council, in pursuance of the government's advice to rationalise, decided to close the prestigious Paisley Grammar school.

The decision prompted a national newspaper to start a campaign which, in turn, led to the intervention of the Prime Minister. The consequence of this was that the Secretary of State for Scotland then got parliamentary approval to change education legislation so that school closures should be referred to him where the school roll was over 80 per cent capacity. The local authorities' decision-making powers had thus been further restricted.

The School Boards (Scotland) Act 1988, coming into force in April 1989, requires local education authorities to set up school boards, and proposed legislation, the Self-Governing Schools Etc. (Scotland) Bill, will allow these boards to decide if they wish to "opt out" of the local authority sector. These new features of the educational scene will be discussed later.

The non-compulsory sector of local authority educational provision is very diverse. Pre-school provision is often referred to as nursery education but a complicating factor here is that there are two departments (and committees) involved in this. The education department is normally involved in providing nursery classes for those over three years old—these take place in the normal school hours and are the responsibility of a qualified teacher. These nursery classes are often in the same building as the primary school, thus ensuring a smooth transition from non-compulsory to compulsory education.

Day nurseries and play groups are the responsibility of the social work department. Day nurseries have longer hours than nursery schools and can take children from only a few months to school entry age. These are in the charge of qualified social workers or nursery nurses. Play groups are usually groups of individuals who come together to provide some sort of daytime activity for pre-school children, and local authority social work departments will often give these groups grants. It must be noted that there is no statutory obligation on a local authority to provide pre-school facilities or services in its area.

Post-school education is very wide-ranging. Between the ages of 16 and 18 most post-school education actually takes place in schools where pupils stay on to complete their secondary education by sitting the Scottish Certificate of Education examinations. However, local authorities also provide for post-school education in further education colleges. Increasingly now this FE sector is dividing up into "advanced" and "non-advanced"—the Scottish Education Department's terminology. Non-advanced FE normally ends with qualifications equivalent to the Scottish National Certificates of SCOTVEC or the City and Guilds of London. Students enter these courses with "O" grades (Standard grade from 1990–91) or simply on leaving school at 16.

Advanced FE is very complicated but normally entrance to these courses will require "Higher" grades, and students take HND or HNC courses and may enter degree courses with qualifications given by the Council for National Academic Awards. As a rough guide non-advanced FE starts at 16 and is normally completed by 19 or 20, while advanced FE starts about 18 and is normally completed by 21 or 22 (thus overlapping with university provision).

The trend in further education in recent years has been to allow certain colleges to "opt out" of the local authority sector. Thus Glasgow College and Napier Polytechnic, Edinburgh, became Central Institutions directly financed by the Scottish Education Department. Ministerial thinking seems to be moving in the direction of allowing other types of further education colleges the right to "opt out" in the same manner as the above colleges and within the legislation allowing schools to "opt out".

Local education authorities also provide other post-school educational opportunities. This sector used to be called non-formal or adult education but since the Alexander report of 1974 has been known as community education. This embraces the various evening classes in subjects ranging from archaeology to Zen Buddhism. In recent years also there have been developments which allow adults to participate in secondary school classes along with pupils, particularly if the adult is studying for a Scottish Certificate of Education examination. Local authorities charge fees for this part of the education system although these classes are highly subsidised.

Apart from nursery education (where some local authority expenditure is repaid through the revenue support grant) and staying-on education in secondary schools, the non-compulsory sector of education is largely paid for from the community charge and non-domestic rates. This means that in periods of local authority cuts in expenditure the non-compulsory sector of education may have to suffer more than the compulsory sector.

Education authorities also provide what might be described as non-educational services. For instances there are special services such as school health (including school dentists), school meals (including milk), child guidance services, special provision for mentally and physically handicapped children, school transport, and school library services.

The private sector of education has always been smaller in Scotland than in the rest of the United Kingdom. However, recent legislation and Conservative government proposals are designed to encourage the growth of this area at the expense, some would argue, of the public sector. The Assisted Places Scheme was introduced in 1981 to allow children of "low income" families to gain access to private education. The Self Governing Schools Etc. (Scotland) Bill will also allow the new school boards, described in chapter 4, to "opt out" of the local authority sector. This will not make them private schools because they will still be financed from the public sector. Some commentators have argued that these developments will "cream off" good pupils to the private or "opted out" sector at the expense of the public sector.

The Conservative government also intends to legislate for a new type of school to be called "technology academies". These will be for pupils over the age of 15 who show "aptitude and commitment" in the technology fields. The start-up costs of the schools will be borne by the Scottish Education Department but it is expected that local businesses will bear the running costs. Although these schools will not charge fees, once again, some authorities fear that they will "cream off" talent from the public education system.

Social Work

Education may be regarded as one of the older local authority services but social work is undoubtedly one of the new services. Prior to 1969 burghs and county councils shared responsibilities for child welfare and general welfare in the community. The Social Work (Scotland) Act 1968 however redefined social work and since 1975 this has been a regional responsibility.

The Act confers on regional (and islands) authorities a general duty to promote social welfare in their areas. This is often seen as having a responsibility for "vulnerable" groups, e.g. children in need of care, old people, the mentally and physically handicapped, but the Act is much more general than this, allowing local authorities a measure of responsibility for communities which may have special problems. The wording of the Act is very comprehensive:

> "It shall be the duty of every local authority to promote social welfare by making available advice, guidance and assistance on such a scale as may be appropriate for their area" (s. 12(1)).

Given this comprehensiveness it is less easy to describe the range of work encompassed by the term "social work" than it is to define the term "education". By the very nature of the work much will depend on individual and local circumstances. In many ways it could be easier to describe social work as taking on the problems which are not the direct responsibility of other local government services or national government departments and agencies.

A brief description of social work cannot do justice to the wide range of activities of a social work department but we can best see this in terms of groups. Local authority social work responsibilities include children "at risk", i.e. those who have little or no parental care. Authorities will provide residential or day facilities for these children either through group homes or fostering. Although the children's panel or hearing system is not strictly the responsibility of local authorities, social work (and education) departments are closely involved in the work of these panels. As has previously been mentioned, social work departments have responsibilities for day nurseries, children's homes and residential nurseries, together with concern for pre-school playgroups.

In terms of family care the work of the departments here covers general support and financial assistance, homes for mothers and babies, home helps, temporary accommodation and responsibilities for homelessness. This latter responsibility cuts across local government services, since homeless persons are the responsibility of social work departments but the provision of a house (or a roof) is the responsibility of housing departments. However since reorganisation local authorities have developed liaison (or joint) committees between social work and housing to resolve difficulties and ensure that those at risk do not suffer from the divided responsibilities.

The mentally and physically disabled are also looked after by social work departments who invariably try to keep a register of these groups of people and provide homes, care, day centres, training and employment. This type of care often overlaps with care for the elderly. In this respect "meals on wheels" and "lunch clubs" are a regular feature of many community centres. Other types of care for the elderly include home helps, day centres, clubs for the elderly and homes for the elderly.

Amongst what might be regarded as miscellaneous social work provision would be the supervision and after-care of adults on probation and the provision of hostels and lodging houses for single (mostly unemployable) people.

It is obvious from the above description that any social work department has to have strong links with other personal services, with voluntary agencies and local health authorities. Official thinking for the 1990s seems to suggest that community care will replace hospital care. This will increase the role and responsibilities of social work departments. It may seem that this development, reviewed in the Scottish Health Service Planning Council's Report "Scottish Health Authorities Review of Priorities for the Eighties and Nineties" (the SHARPEN report), would create overlap and duplication between the community roles of social work departments and local health boards. However it must be remembered that the health boards are concerned with the medical and clinical aspects of their clients, while the social work departments are only concerned with their responsibilities under the Social Work Act. Nevertheless the SHARPEN report did recommend that there should be joint teams to look after clients at risk in the community. At the time of writing, however, there is no indication that central government will financially support the added responsibilities of local authorities.

Planning

Planning is a "concurrent function" although the 1973 Act attempts to define the boundaries of responsibilities. Leaving aside any consideration of policy planning which will be discussed later, "planning" here means physical planning and includes strategic planning and local planning.

Strategic planning is a regional and islands responsibility and includes research and intelligence, strategic economic planning, land use planning, industrial and urban development and the countryside. Under the 1973 Act and various Town and Country Planning Acts the regional (and islands) authorities have a responsibility to produce a "structure plan". This plan is based on population trends and is concerned not only with the size of the population but its location. The aim of the structure plan is to try to set objectives for *all* the local government services in each region and as such is concerned with what economists would call "resource allocation". By its very nature therefore, strategic planning is about infrastructure, but because of this it impinges on services provided by district authorities, particularly housing.

Both in the Wheatley Report and the 1973 Act recognition was made that some district authorities would be too small to deal with even local planning. For this reason local planning, development control, urban redevelopment, building control, listed buildings and conservation areas are the responsibility of the regional authorities in the Highland, Borders and Dumfries and Galloway Regions. However, in these areas the regions have devised an organisation whereby the district authorities (members and officials) are involved in local planning decisions by means of a type of liaison committee. The above regions and the island authorities are usually described as general planning authorities.

The Protective Services

The Wheatley Report linked police, fire and civil defence together under this classification because:

> "they all have a common purpose in dealing with emergency situations and seeking to maintain or restore public order. Furthermore, they have a common character in that each requires a disciplined force" (para. 475).

Looking at the nature and control of the police service it is difficult to establish it as a local government service. Local authorities (regions and islands) are virtually without influence on the policing of an area because they cannot interfere in operational matters. The main responsibility of a local authority in this respect is in equipping the police force and ensuring its proper administration.

In reality the Secretary of State for Scotland has more direct power over police forces than do local authorities, because the

Secretary of State's responsibilities are to ensure that police forces are run efficiently. It is because of this that central government bears most of the cost of police forces in Scotland and the Secretary of State's approval is required for the appointment of all chief constables and deputy and assistant chief constables.

Despite the considerable powers of the Secretary of State in respect of police services, it was the recommendation of the Wheatley commission that these services should remain part of the local government system, thus reiterating the recommendation of the Royal Commission on the Police in 1962. The reasons for this conclusion were that the police should be seen as a community service and that there were strong links between the police and other local authority services like social work and traffic management.

Unlike the police, the fire service is much more a local government service. Here the local authority has power to vary the establishment, appoint senior officers, control equipment and buildings and concern itself with operational aspects. Because the local authority has more power over fire services, the Secretary of State has less power and consequently central government interference (and money) is less also.

Transportation

The Wheatley report described services under this heading as including:

> "building highways and bridges, maintaining street lighting, providing fleets of buses . . . meeting daily crises in traffic flow and commuter services . . . and involving heavy expenditure, both capital and current" (para. 233).

This description shows the diverse nature of transportation and, as the Wheatley report pointed out, there is a strong connection between transportation and planning. Regional and islands authorities have other transport responsibilities in addition to the above and this includes being involved with other "providing" authorities like the Scottish Transport Group, the various ports authorities, the Civil Airports Authority and British Rail. When this is realised, the difficulties of local authorities in planning transportation become apparent.

Because of the need for transportation planning, regional and islands authorities are required to produce a transport policies and programme document, or "TPP", which covers policy on road building, car parking provision, bus routes and integration with other transport providers. This document can be the subject of public discussion and, if necessary, inquiry. It is updated each year. Obviously, such an exercise is closely linked with the production of a structure plan. However with the deregulation, and even privatisation, of bus undertakings it has to be doubted how much weight the TPP has, given that even roadbuilding policy is mostly determined by the central government.

In terms of transport operations local authority powers have been reduced in recent years. The city bus services operated by Strathclyde, Lothian, Tayside and Grampian Regional Councils were "deregulated" in 1985. This meant that running of city bus services was handed over to private companies albeit that all the shares in that company were owned by the respective regional authorities. At the time of writing Grampian Transport has been bought by its employees and managers and the government has indicated that it would like this to happen to the other regional transport companies.

Thus local authorities have lost direct control of bus services and the monopoly of city bus services has ended. Other private companies can bid to the regional authorities for certain or all of the routes in the city. Apart from this "opening tenders" aspect, the only direct input to transport is where a regional authority, through its social work budget, may give a subsidy to the transport company to reduce or abolish fares for the elderly. Perhaps the title "transportation committee" has become a misnomer.

A recent report on British bus services indicated that deregulation had not significantly improved fares or services.

Water, Sewerage, etc.

Under this heading is included water supply, sewerage, river purification and flood prevention. These are essential services for the infrastructure of areas, but since they are determined largely by geographical rather than administrative boundaries it is often not easy to fit them into any structure of local government.

Water supply is a particularly difficult service to give administrative boundaries to, and this is illustrated by the fact that over recent years this has been the responsibility of local authorities, joint authorities, water boards and now regional authorities. The difficulty arises where the source of a water supply may well be in another local authority's area, resulting in the possibility of supply pipes being duplicated or overlapping. For the same reason the building of reservoirs is a costly and lengthy undertaking which requires separate financing. Added to this is the fact that many industrial and commercial users have to pay more or may be metered. This means that there has to be a water charge levied separately from the community charge or non-domestic rate.

Although the previous water boards were abolished and regions took over water supply, this was not the case with river pollution. The old river purification boards were abolished but new boards were set up. The representation on the new boards was one-third from the regions in the area, one-third from the districts in the area, and one-third appointed by the Secretary of State for Scotland to represent the various interests in the board's area.

The Conservative government announced in 1987 that it was proposing to privatise the various water authorities in England and Wales, and the Water Bill now before Parliament will implement this, but at the time of writing there has been no announcement of a similar proposal for Scotland.

District Functions
Housing

Housing is probably the major function of district councils, although the Wheatley commission felt that it should be a regional responsibility, mainly because of its close links with social work. The Conservative government, in passing the 1973 Act felt, however, that the district councils would be too weak if they were not given a major responsibility.

The responsibilities of housing authorities fall into three categories—assessment of need, building operations and management. Currently housing authorities have to submit to the Secretary of State for Scotland housing plans, which basically are forward plans as to how the local authorities see the housing needs in their areas being met. This means that housing authorities have overall responsibility for housing policy in their area and are not just concerned, as many think, with council houses.

Assessment of need is a very wide responsibility for housing authorities, since it requires gathering information about how people are housed and what demand there might be for all types of public and private housing in their area. Such an exercise also requires local authorities to assess housing conditions. In this respect the central government lays down a minimum acceptable standard—the tolerable standard. Housing authorities will then have to decide what to do with houses which are "below the tolerable standard". To demolish requires that the inhabitants have to be rehoused and the ability of a local authority to do this is determined by the availability of houses in the area.

If there is a shortfall between supply and demand the local authority will have to decide how this can be made up. Leaving aside the private housebuilding sector over which the local authority has little control, except perhaps by making land available and designating residential land through the structure and local plan system, the authority has two options—build new houses or improve existing houses.

The building of new houses by a local authority has been severely restricted in recent years as a consequence of two factors—Conservative government policy and the response of Labour district councils (the majority of district councils) who have opposed these policies. The government's view has been based on three principles: first, that council house rents in Scotland were too low; secondly, that tenants should be encouraged to buy their council houses, and thirdly, encouraging the private rented sector.

Housing finance will be dealt with in Chapter 5 but it should be pointed out here that housing accounts are required to be kept separate from the accounts of the rest of the authority's services (general services). Successive governments have tried to persuade local authorities to balance their housing accounts without resorting to subsidies from the revenue accounts. In other words council housing should be self-financing. Central government has continually limited these subsidies to the housing account and the housing capital allocation became restricted or disappeared altogether. Added to this was the defiance of some councils, notably Edinburgh, who refused to raise rents to meet the shortfall in subsidies. The consequence of these events was that many local authorities had no money to build new council houses or provide adequate maintenance or management services.

The government's policy of encouraging council house sales has also had its consequences on house building. By giving considerable discounts (sometimes up to 70 per cent) to sitting tenants to buy their houses this reduced the stock of "good" houses, i.e. those requiring less maintenance costs and those in the more desirable areas. However the local authority had borrowed money on the 100 per cent cost when building the houses and still had to pay back the original loan. Further, the housing stock which remained was generally of the older type and required more maintenance. Added to that was the loss of rents from the houses which had been sold. Councils, therefore, found it difficult to raise capital for new houses when so much of their housing (rents) had to go simply to keep the housing revenue account in balance.

With the difficulties of building new houses, central government has been encouraging local authorities to move in two other directions, either to help improve older houses or enter into "joint venture" housing with the private building sector.

Nowadays local authorities have three methods of improving older houses—grants and loans to owners, improvement of the housing authorities' own houses or the buying up of old houses and the handing over of these to housing associations. All of this is often described as rehabilitation. Housing associations are groups of owners and tenants in an area who receive grants from Scottish Homes (formerly the Housing Corporation) to improve their property on a collective basis. This mainly applies to tenement property.

With little or no capital for council house building, many councils were forced to come to some sort of arrangement with the private sector if houses were to be built at all. Since local authorities own a considerable amount of land, the solution was an arrangement where the council supplied the land and the builder built the houses either for sale or for cost rent. In either case the houses are outside the council's ownership and control.

One other method of providing houses should be mentioned here. Central government has been trying to persuade local authorities to hand over houses to Scottish Homes which then, in turn, funds tenant co-operatives or housing associations. Although the local authority may retain some nomination rights for a certain number of its tenants, the houses are no longer owned by the authority.

The third responsibility of housing authorities is the maintenance and management of its own stock of houses. Local authorities are usually the largest landlords in an area, and as such have the normal duties and responsibilities of a landlord, i.e. to keep their property in good repair. Due to the restrictions put on subsidies to the housing account, many local authorities have found it difficult to meet their obligation to maintain property, resulting in "void" houses, i.e. houses without tenants. If the authority cannot repair these houses they may remain empty for long periods with a consequent loss of rents, thus exacerbating the problem. In addition to this, housing authorities have a responsibility in the area of estate management—trying to keep the environment (fences, grassed areas, etc.) in good order. As landlords, housing authorities are also concerned with rent collection, with transferring tenants from house to house if the tenants wish to transfer, and, more recently, with the administration of the central government's housing benefit scheme. It is in this last area that the overlap with social work services occurs.

Perhaps the best way of clarifying the "grey area" between housing and social work is to say that housing departments often see themselves as simply concerned with "bricks and mortar"—

the tenants (and their problems) are therefore the responsibility of the social work department. As the Wheatley report said:

"considered strictly on their own [allocation and management] might not require such large authorities. But they cannot be considered strictly on their own. They are linked intimately with both house building and with personal social services" (para. 472).

It is because of this link, and the allocation of housing and social work to different tiers, that problems have arisen since local government reform. An attempt to solve the problem was made with the Morris report which advocated liaison committees between regions and districts to iron out problems between housing and social work. However the problem was highlighted by the plight of homeless persons. These were obviously the responsibility of the social work department but their need for a house could only be met by the housing authority. An added difficulty in some areas was where the two authorities were of different political complexions, and the homeless person then became a political football.

The Housing (Homeless Persons) Act 1977, as consolidated in the Housing (Scotland) Act 1987, gave the responsibility of providing a roof for a homeless person to the housing authority, but problems still exist where there is a shortage of accommodation. There is also a problem of what is meant by "providing a roof". Standards of accommodation vary considerably between local authorities depending on availability of suitable accommodation. Thus approaches to dealing with homelessness can vary considerably throughout Scotland.

As mentioned earlier, housing authorities are not just concerned with their own houses. Under a variety of housing and public health legislation local authorities can control conditions for private tenants, particularly in multi-occupancy houses. A recent case in Edinburgh gave the local authority power to take over a house from the landlord, although on that occasion it was not housing but public health legislation which was used.

A further recent development in council housing took place as a consequence of the Housing (Scotland) Act 1988. This Act reflects the Conservative government's philosophy that housing, in a sense, should be privatised from local authorities. Under this legislation tenants are given the right, in addition to their right to buy, to choose a landlord other than the local authority, so long as that landlord is registered with Scottish Homes as a suitable landlord.

This development has to be seen alongside other provisions of the same Act which created Scottish Homes, a public agency, to take on the responsibilities of the former Housing Corporation and the Scottish Special Housing Association. This new agency can become a landlord, not for individual tenants, but for groups of tenants, in part or all of a council housing estate, who might want to opt for Scottish Homes as their landlord.

The new legislation also allows for groups of tenants to opt, if they so wish, for a private landlord or to form a housing co-operative by collectively buying their houses from the local authority.

As can be seen from the above details, there will be a profound change during the next few years in council housing which will considerably reduce a local authority's housing responsibilities, although they will retain a strategic role with regard to housing in their area. Not surprisingly local authorities have seen these developments as a further reduction of their powers.

Environmental Services

The responsibilities in this category of services are diverse but are mainly concerned with creating a good environment, and some of the services here are fundamental to urban living. The functions included here are cleansing and refuse collection; baths and washhouses; regulation of shops, offices, markets and slaughter-houses; food hygiene, and burial and cremation. In the past these were often described as public health.

Cleansing and refuse disposal include street cleaning and refuse collection and disposal. Although all these aspects are important it is refuse disposal which is a big expenditure item to local authorities. The extent of modern packaging is such that more equipment is required to cope with this. However, recent years have seen an increased interest in recycling of waste or packaging materials and local authorities are only too conscious of their responsibilities in this area. There is an attraction to a local authority to reduce costs of collection by separation of different types of waste material—bottles, waste paper, metal, etc. and many authorities have been investing heavily in this.

With modern standards of house building the provision of baths and washhouses may be seen as an anachronism. However it must be remembered that so long as there are older houses in areas and older people who may not be able to afford washing machines, there is still need for these services. Many local authorities, in an effort to make the best use of these facilities, have upgraded them to try to meet competition from commercial launderettes.

Local authorities have considerable statutory powers and responsibilities in respect of the regulation of public premises and standards of food hygiene. Here the local authority will inspect premises regularly and also investigate complaints from members of the public. This type of service is done unobtrusively, but it is often taken for granted by the public, who would soon complain if standards were to be lowered or if there was not adequate inspection particularly of food shops, restaurants, public houses, etc.

Recently many environmental health authorities have taken on the responsibility for pollution monitoring, particularly radiation monitoring following the Chernobyl accident in 1986, together with concern about leakage from domestic or military nuclear establishments.

Recreation

The Wheatley report described the services under this heading as "amenity functions", but most local authorities now describe them as "recreation" or "recreation and leisure" services. The range of provision here includes parks, sports centres, swimming pools, museums, art galleries and often municipal theatres.

As with environmental health, local authorities have brought these diverse activities under one department and committee in accordance with the principles of corporate management. However the scale of these activities and past tradition has often meant that district authorities do not carry out all the above services. Most districts are involved in public parks and the maintenance and management of these, but the provision of sports centres and swimming pools can be costly and although responsibility for these has resided with the districts since 1982, some districts have sought the help of regions to provide these where they can be attached to school provision.

Much the same can be said about libraries, museums and art galleries. Indeed in the Highland, Borders and Dumfries and Galloway Regions, it was found impossible to separate libraries from the education service and consequently this is a regional function. It is obvious that the services for what is often described as "cultural recreation" are even more connected to education. As with physical recreation, even where the districts are the providers it is schoolchildren and students who will be the main consumers.

Once again the Conservative government's stated intentions affect the recreational functions of local authorities. There is evidence to suggest that privatisation of recreational services is being considered in England and Wales and, if this should happen, it is more than likely that Scotland will follow.

The Local Government Act 1988 allowed for certain "defined activities" to be put out to tender as will be explained at the end of this chapter. Although sports and leisure management were not mentioned in the original Bill, the Government subsequently added these and local authorities will be required, but not before 1992, to put the management of such recreational facilities out to tender.

Planning

A district council's responsibility for planning includes local land use and development control. As mentioned earlier, general planning authorities also have these responsibilities but usually decentralise consideration of local planning applications to divisional authorities based on district boundaries. In this section we shall simply refer to districts. Legislation requires district planning authorities to prepare local plans, each of which has to fit into the broad approach of the structure plan.

There are three types of local plans. District plans cover all or part of a district authority's area. The broad strategy is laid out in the structure plan and the details for implementation are set out in this local plan. In small districts there may only be one plan for the area whereas larger districts will probably be broken up into a number of area plans. Action area plans are usually designated in the structure plan as areas requiring improvement or redevelopment. Subject plans are those which explain policy on a particular subject such as commercial development, industrial estates or tourist facilities. Obviously the drawing up of all of these plans requires very close consultation between regions and districts.

Development control is concerned with the change of use of land and buildings and encompasses anything from house extensions to major town centre development and advertisements to tree preservation. It is not necessary to go into detailed description of the procedure for planning applications. Broadly speaking developers will submit their application to the district (or general) planning authority. There are statutory requirements to inform interested parties such as neighbours. Council officials will usually discuss problems with the developer and explain council policy, e.g. style of windows, limits on the height of buildings, and what is acceptable in a conservation area. In the larger type of development there may also have to be discussions with regional officials about, for instance, impact on parking and road safety.

The planning committee will then discuss the proposal. Before this stage is reached it is likely that councillors will have been "lobbied" by both supporters of and objectors to the proposal. The committee has delegated powers to make final decisions. The committee can make one of three decisions. Permission may be granted, refused or granted subject to conditions. In the case of refusal the reasons for that refusal must be on planning grounds based in the Planning Acts and not on political (or whimsical) grounds. If an application is refused or granted conditionally the developer has the right of appeal to the Secretary of State for Scotland.

The Secretary of State may approve, refuse or set up a public inquiry. Whatever decision the Secretary of State makes overrides the planning authority decision and there is no appeal except to the courts on a point of law. Under the 1973 Act, regional authorities have the power to "call in", i.e. to consider and veto (if necessary) planning applications if the region believes that the proposed development is contrary to the objectives of the structure plan. In addition the Secretary of State for Scotland has the power to "call in" any planning application if he thinks the development would affect central government policy or where there might be conflict between two regional authorities.

There has been controversy recently about the use of the "green belt". The post-war Planning Acts designated areas around cities as "green belts" where it was expected that no further developments should take place. This was to provide a "lung" for city dwellers within easy reach of a city centre. Throughout the post-war years, however, local authorities have come under considerable pressure to release land in the "green belt" mainly for housing development. It is argued that releasing some of this land reduces land (and therefore house) prices. The counter argument is that allowing encroachments on the "green belt" will increase urbanisation and reduce leisure activities. Conservative Secretaries of State in recent years have tended to allow certain encroachments on the green belt if they have felt this would reduce house prices but have balanced this with certain conditions about the number of houses per hectare. However, overall it would appear that reductions of the "green belt" have been compensated for by taking in land previously undesignated, thus keeping a rough balance.

Planning laws and regulations are continually being amended and updated. However the general principles are as set out in the Local Government (Scotland) Act 1973. The Conservative government in 1988 issued a consultation document proposing that the planning laws be loosened up. The stated aim was to speed up development mainly in the towns and cities. It would mean, for instance, that certain properties could change their use without requiring planning permission from the local authority. As an example a restaurant could be changed into a public house without local authority consent. Not surprisingly many local authorities see these proposals as a further erosion of their powers. At the time of writing no legislation has been brought forward.

Islands Functions

The Wheatley report had not envisioned any islands authorities, mainly on the grounds that these areas were too small to function on their own, but as indicated earlier, the Conservative government in 1973 allowed for three islands councils which were to be "most purpose" authorities. This meant that although they controlled many local government services they, for reasons of efficiency, had to be amalgamated with another regional authority for certain other services. However to all intents and purposes they are equivalent to regional authorities albeit that they are "single tier".

These islands areas of Orkney, Shetland and the Western Isles are amalgamated with the Highland Region for police and fire services. For valuation purposes Orkney and Shetland Islands Councils combine, as do Highland Region and Western Isles councils. Because there was some disquiet about this arrangement the government set up a committee of inquiry in 1982, the Montgomery committee. The remit covered other aspects of the islands areas such as their constitutional relationship with the United Kingdom and the restrictions placed on oil revenues by the government but, as regards local authority functions, the report, published in 1984, suggested that the system was working well and did not recommend any change.

The Convention of Scottish Local Authorities

Before 1975 there was no one voice which spoke for the interests of local authorities. There were instead four national organisations which reflected the structure of the old local government system, the oldest of which was the Convention of Royal Burghs. When reorganisation was imminent in 1975 it appeared as if there would be, again, no one organisation for Scottish local authorities, partly because of traditional jealousies and partly because of the differing functions and powers of the new regional authorities. However self interest was put aside although perhaps at the expense of a complicated structure of checks and balances in the new organis-ation.

The main objectives of COSLA are threefold. First, to protect and promote the interests and the rights of the member authorities, particularly with regard to proposed legislation. Secondly, to act as a discussion forum for matters of mutual interest to the local authorities. In this respect it acts as a "clearing house" of information by collecting the views of its members and conveying these views to other local authority organisations (in the UK) or to the government. Thirdly, it is concerned with providing essential services, like the National Joint Council (on wages) and training information, to the member authorities.

The structure of the convention is complex but basically there are three types of committees. First, are those committees which are concerned with district (and islands) functions, e.g. housing, arts and recreation, etc. Secondly, there are those committees dealing with regional (and islands) functions, e.g. education, social work, roads and transport, etc. Finally, there are joint committees dealing with convention policy, personnel and planning. Membership of committees is structured so that the larger authorities do not overwhelm the smaller authorities. In this sense the smaller authorities are over-represented. However when it comes to financing the convention, the contribution of each local authority is based on population.

Much of the work of the convention is concerned with matters arising from legislation and government policy. In this sense it acts as an adviser to the government. This is particularly so when it comes to the various grant settlements each year. Another aspect of the convention's work is to try to get standards laid down so that there is not too much variation in the provision of services between one local authority and another. However, any recommendation from COSLA to member authorities is only advisory and not obligatory.

Because the Conservative government has been more active in producing legislation on local government and because many of the local authorities in Scotland are Labour controlled, COSLA has been more active in the campaigning sense. This was particularly evident over the legislation creating the community charge. The "higher profile" of COSLA has brought about accusations both from inside and outside the convention that it has become "political". COSLA's response has simply been that it is reflecting the views of its members.

New and Proposed Legislation
Since the first edition of this book there has been a considerable increase in legislation relating to local authorities. Some of that legislation has already been mentioned and other legislation will be described in its appropriate place in the book. Here we will

summarise the more important Acts affecting the functions and responsibilities of Scottish local authorities. In addition, as this book is going to press, the government is proposing further legislation.

The two most important Acts affecting the functions of Scottish local authorities are the Housing (Scotland) Act 1987 and the Local Government Act 1988. The Housing Act is a consolidation of existing statutes and covers the powers and duties of local authorities, homeless persons, rights of public sector tenants, housing accounts and government grants and subsidies. Some of these features have been referred to in this chapter and the financial aspects will be dealt with in Chapter 5. However the Housing (Scotland) Act 1988 now contains the far-reaching provision to abolish the Housing Corporation in Scotland and the Scottish Special Housing Association (SSHA). These agencies were replaced, on 1 April 1989, by Scottish Homes which took over their responsibilities, including being landlord for SSHA houses. Although district councils pressed the government to transfer SSHA houses to their housing stock this proposal was rejected, underlining many councils' suspicions that the new Scottish Homes would sell off their houses to private companies. So far Scottish Homes has denied that it will do this although it remains open to the idea of selling off the houses to housing associations or tenant co-operatives.

The Local Government Act 1988 applies to England, Wales and Scotland. Its main provisions relate to the introduction of compulsory competitive tendering (CCT) in certain local government services. The government believes that CCT will improve the efficiency of local government services and lead to value for money. The Act lists activities which are to be exposed to competition. These "defined activities" include:

- building cleaning
- street cleaning
- school and welfare catering
- other catering
- maintenance of ground
- repair and maintenance of vehicles.

The Act allows the Secretary of State to add further activities to the list and, indeed, at the end of 1988, sport and leisure management were added. All activities with a gross cost of over £100,000 are to be open to tender. CCT will be phased in both by activity and by council. In other words some councils will be implementing CCT in, say, street cleaning earlier than others. It is obvious that this Act will profoundly affect the functions and decision-making powers of local authorities.

At the beginning of 1989 the government introduced yet more local government legislation. At the time of writing this legislation has not been enacted but the Local Government and Housing Bill is mostly concerned with the recommendations of the Widdicombe report which will be dealt with in the next chapter. However there is one aspect of the Bill which relates to council functions. The housing clauses allow local authorities to sell off all their housing stock if they so wish. In addition there are provisions about housing finance which will be dealt with in Chapter 5.

CHAPTER 3

COUNCILLORS, COMMITTEES AND DEPARTMENTS

As was mentioned in Chapter 1, local government in Scotland has a long history preceding a structured central administration. However until the nineteenth century its personnel could not be described as representative of the local citizens. Even in the nineteenth century councillors were elected by a minority of the citizens. Thus, in a sense, increased powers for local authorities in the twentieth century have matched the increasing size of the electorate. As the electorate increased in numbers so the need to organise election campaigns grew. Although political parties were organised at parliamentary elections they were slow to develop in local elections. In effect party politics in local government is a very recent development.

As the powers and responsibilities of local councils grew so it was necessary to organise the business of the council. Unlike the parliamentary system, and perhaps because of the low profile of party politics, local authorities developed a committee system and not a cabinet system, with departmental officials responsible to a committee rather than to a minister as in the Westminster model. Despite attempts at reforming that committee system it remains the basic structure of Scottish local government.

Elections

Local government elections have attracted their share of criticism because of low turnout and the intrusion of "national politics". Despite this the procedures used have changed very little. Much of the legislation on qualifications and procedures has survived local government reform and only arrangements for boundary changes have altered with the creation of the Local Government Boundary Commission.

Voting qualifications for local elections do not significantly differ from qualifications for parliamentary elections. Those entitled to be registered and to vote must be:
(a) resident in the local authority area on the qualifying date (usually October 10 each year);
(b) not subject to any legal incapacity to vote, and either a British subject or a citizen of the Republic of Ireland; and
(c) of voting age, on the date of the poll, i.e. 18 years or over.
Those who are not 18 by the date the register is published

30

(February 15) but who will reach that age during the currency of the register have the date of their birthday against their name and can vote at any election taking place on or after their birthday.

Certain categories of electors are entitled to vote by post. Electors who are unable to vote in person because of their occupation or employment or because of blindness or other physical incapacity, or because they would have to make a journey by sea or air *from their qualifying address* to the polling station can apply to vote by post. Since 1985 the rules for postal voting have been extended to include those on holiday on polling day and the returning officer has more discretion about who qualifies for a postal vote. Applications for a postal vote must be received by the last day for nomination.

Proxy voting is restricted. Only electors who have appointed a proxy for parliamentary elections can appoint a proxy for local elections. Only two categories of electors can appoint proxies.

(a) civilians whose employment takes them to sea or abroad;
(b) persons registered as service voters—these include
    servicemen, Crown servants and British Council employees.

No person can be specially appointed as proxy for local government elections.

Election procedure is fairly well established in Scottish local government and is contained in the Representation of the People Act 1983 and supplemented by various Statutory Instruments issued from time to time. The preliminary procedures are determined by the election day (normally the first Thursday in May; occasionally the second). Nominations close on the fourth Tuesday preceding election day. Notice of withdrawals must be made by the third Thursday preceding election day. Nominations of polling and counting agents are made on the Thursday preceding election day. Candidate nominations require two proposers and eight others. Together with the names of the candidate a "description not exceeding six words" is allowed. This permits candidates to put the name of the political party which they are representing.

Candidates normally appoint an election agent although they can act as their own agent. It is the agent's responsibility to deal with all the legal and financial arrangements for the election and it is the agent who is held responsible if election law is breached. In addition to these procedural responsibilities the election agent will organise most aspects of the candidate's campaign including the raising of sufficient money.

The cost of an election campaign is limited by law. For local government elections this limit is currently set at £150 plus 3p for each entry on the electoral register in each ward. Candidates, however, are allowed free use of schools for public meetings, though they are not allowed free distribution of election addresses as in parliamentary elections. There are certain requirements laid down about the campaign, e.g. committee rooms cannot be in a polling station; all literature must have the name of an election agent; no canvassing or loudspeakers are allowed outside polling stations.

On election day the hours of polling are 8.00 a.m. to 9.00 p.m. and are now the same for all local authorities. There is no provision for an extension of hours. In addition to an election agent each candidate is allowed to appoint polling agents. The number of polling agents is usually laid down by the returning officer. Polling agents act as the candidate's agent at the polling stations. Only candidates, their election agent and polling agents are allowed to attend polling stations to check for personation, etc.

Procedure at the counting of ballot papers is uniform. The ballot boxes are first sealed and then conveyed to the central counting station. At the central counting station the total votes cast are counted first and checked against the counterfoils. This is to ensure that no ballot papers have been lost (or added!). Each candidate's votes are then counted (usually in bundles of 100) and doubtful ballot papers, e.g. the "X" overlapping two names, are adjudicated by candidates and the presiding officer. Each candidate is allowed a prescribed number of counting agents—the number is laid down by the returning officer—who ensure that the proper procedure is carried out by the counting clerks. Ballot papers and "marked registers" (which give a record of those who have voted although not how they voted) are kept for six months and then destroyed.

Councillors

Councillors have also come in for criticism since local government reform with claims that they have become too "professional" and "political". Nevertheless there are still standard requirements which councillors have to adhere to and these, as in the elections, have changed little over the years.

There are certain qualifications necessary to be elected as a councillor. A candidate must be 21 years old or more (note that the voting age is 18 years); be a British subject or citizen of the Irish Republic; be a local government elector within the area of the local authority or have resided or have their principal place of work in the area of the authority for 12 months preceding their nomination.

There are also a number of factors which disqualify a person from standing for election in local government. Persons who hold a paid office at the disposal of the local authority or of a joint committee to which the authority is party are disqualified, as are persons who are undischarged bankrupts or who have been disqualified for corrupt or illegal practices.

Once in office councillors have certain legal obligations. If a member of a local authority fails, through a period of six consecutive months, to attend any meeting of the authority he shall, unless the authority has approved of such absence, cease to be a councillor. Vacancies, by death or resignation, are filled by a by-election except if such vacancy occurs within six months of the next ordinary election of the council. A person filling a casual vacancy holds office only until the next ordinary election.

Other legal obligations pertain to financial interest and sur-charge. Numerous Acts and regulations set out procedures for financial interest. The main provisions are in regard to pecuniary and non-pecuniary interests. With regard to pecuniary interests the member must declare an interest and refrain from taking part in the discussion and any vote on the matter. Breach of these requirements is a criminal offence. Non-pecuniary interests are less easy to define but include such things as being related to someone tendering for a contract. It is not a criminal offence if no declaration of interest is made but most councillors will declare to be on the safe side. Most local authorities have a register of interests but entries in this are not compulsory.

If a member of a local authority authorises the misapplication or improper spending of the authority's funds he can be surcharged and ordered to reimburse the amount misspent. Although such cases are rare there have been recent examples which serve to point to the tension between central and local government.

Allegations of misspending are referred to the Commission for Local Authority Accounts in Scotland—the Accounts Commission. If the Controller of Audit, who is the chief officer of the Commission, after investigating the allegation, believes that there has been misspending he brings this to the attention of the Commission and the local authority concerned. The Commission, who are lay members appointed by the Secretary of State for Scotland, may bring the Secretary of State's attention to the matter. It is then for the Secretary of State to decide what action, if any, should be taken. It is possible for the councillors concerned to challenge the Controller's view in court but such action, in itself, could be construed as misuse of public money.

The recent cases concerned Edinburgh and Stirling District Councils. An interim report by the Widdicombe committee on the conduct of local authority business had recommended a tightening up of legislation on local authority publicity. This resulted in the Local Government Act 1986 which prohibited local authorities from publishing material which appeared to affect public support for the policies of a political party. In 1986 the Controller of Audit believed that Edinburgh had misspent by authorising expenditure on a campaign promoting the council's policies. On that occasion the matter was not referred to the Secretary of State for Scotland and, therefore, no action was taken because the councillors had acted on advice from officials. However in 1988 the Controller maintained that the councillors in Stirling had misspent and the Secretary of State proceeded to surcharge them because they had acted contrary to advice from their officials. It has to be noted here that surcharging, by itself, does not disqualify a councillor but if they refuse or are unable to pay and are, thereafter, declared bankrupt then it is this which disqualifies them.

The Local Government (Scotland) Act 1973 provides for councillors to be paid an attendance allowance for an approved duty. Such payment is for a 24-hour duty. This meant that councillors were paid the same amount whether they attended one five minute meeting or six one-hour meetings within that 24 hours. In the early days of local government reform the attendance allowance system raised some controversy because of the meaning given to "approved duties". The 1973 Act and the Secretary of State allow each local authority to define the types of duties for which it will pay this allowance. The result has been that some local authorities have defined it widely to include meetings with officials, party group meetings, councillors' interviews with constituents, official council receptions, etc.

In the face of this early criticism the government in December 1976 set up a committee of inquiry under the chairmanship of Mr Derek Robinson to review the workings of the attendance allowance system and to make recommendations. The Robinson report, *The Remuneration of Councillors*, was published in 1977 and it pointed to "some serious weaknesses" in the system. Setting its face against salaried councillors, as the Conservative government had done in 1973, the Robinson committee however found it difficult to devise a practical alternative to salaries, attendance allowance and the old financial loss allowance. In the end nothing was done but the discontent continued.

The Stodart committee report referred to in a previous chapter also made comment on the anomalies of the system, and the resulting Local Government and Planning (Scotland) Act 1982 allowed councillors to claim financial loss allowance as an alternative to the attendance allowance. The Secretary of State for

Scotland determines the amount of the attendance allowance, currently a maximum of £18.25 per 24 hours, and financial loss allowance which is currently a maximum of £29.70 per 24 hours or £14.85 per 12 hours. These allowances are subject to tax and national insurance. In addition councils are allowed to give special payments, up to a prescribed limit, for special council responsibilities such as being committee chairperson. Since the Employment Protection Acts of 1975 and 1978 employers are obliged to give "all reasonable" time off for council duties but are not obliged to pay for that time. Public authorities appear to be more generous about paying for time off than do private firms.

Political Parties

There has always been an ambiguous attitude to the role of political parties in the British political system. On the one hand they have been seen as important in mobilising the vote while, on the other hand, they have not, until recently, been recognised in law. Even the Representation of the People Act 1983 does not bend to the recognition of parties but allows candidates to put "a description", not exceeding six words, after their names on the ballot paper.

Political parties in local government have been even less accepted. The tradition that an elected representative serves the public and not a particular sector of the public is even stronger in local government than in national politics. The last section drew attention to the controversy over full-time paid councillors and this underlined the idea of voluntary public service. However, as in national politics, with the growth of the franchise and the growth of an ideological base to politics, party machines have developed since the middle of the nineteenth century. The Labour Party, although late on the scene in national politics, was first on the scene in local politics with its ideas of "municipal socialism" in the 1890s. From then the Labour Party's attitudes to the role of the party in local government fluctuated, depending on its success at the national level. Only after 1945 did the Labour Party intervene extensively in local government resulting in the Conservative Party, with much reluctance, entering the local government arena.

In Scotland, the Labour Party intervened in local government in the urban areas (including large towns) and only very exceptionally in rural areas. This is still very much the case. The Conservatives (or Unionists as they often described themselves) in Scotland were even more reluctant than their English colleagues to enter the fray in local elections, leaving their interests to be promoted by local "Progressives" or "Independents". However, as in 1945, with the return of a Labour government in 1964 the Conservatives in Scotland decided at their conference in 1965 to contest local elections in those areas where the Labour Party was in control.

Since local government reorganisation in 1974–75 political parties have been more in evidence. The reasons for this are quite simple. The new regional authorities have more power and more resources at their disposal. Control of a regional authority is therefore seen, not as an extension of the local party's power, but an adjunct to the national party's effort to control central government.

The Scottish political scene has also recently changed with fluctuating support for the Scottish National Party and the appearance on the electoral scene of the Liberal/Social Democratic Alliance. This electoral alliance of the Liberal Party and the Social Democratic Party merged in 1988 to become the Social and Liberal Democratic Party leaving a rump of the Social Democratic Party, which was the original breakaway from the Labour Party. In addition, what had previously been the Ecology Party, has now become the Green Party. All of these political parties now enter candidates in local elections.

These developments have helped to reinforce political parties in local elections, particularly in the city and large town areas. Thus, despite the misgivings of many people, the fact has to be recognised that political parties have played, and will continue to play, an important role in local government. As the Wheatley report stated:

> "party politics must be accepted as a fact of life. They can neither be legislated for, nor legislated out of existence" (para. 955).

The Council

Many commentators regard the council as a talking-shop or rubber stamp with little power or influence and ruined by the injection of party politics into its deliberations. However, the Wheatley Commission did not share this opinion:

> "We believe . . . that the council should be supreme in the direction and control of the affairs of the authority" (para. 946).

Wheatley went on to distinguish three elements in the supremacy of the council. First, the council is, collectively, the body corporate or legal person—property is vested in the council, staff are appointed by the council, charges are levied by the council and powers delegated to committees are exercised in the name of the council. Secondly, major decisions are taken by the council—the broad policies are set, expenditure approved and the budget debated. Thirdly, the council is a forum for public debate and the challenging and questioning of policy and administration:

"It is in the council chamber that local democracy should be at its most visible" (para. 948).

Council meetings all vary considerably from authority to authority, but within an authority they can also vary. They may be short, uninteresting and uncontroversial but on the other hand they can be long, heated and controversial. Much will depend on factors like political composition, the issues and the interest generated by the public, press or groups.

Let us take two aspects of the full council—those present and the nature of the business transacted. The largest group of those present will be the councillors themselves presided over by the chairman, convener or (lord) provost. Seating patterns vary from council to council and very often depend on party characteristics. Some councils have the continental semi-circular pattern, while others have the parliamentary pattern where the leaders of the two main parties face each other and there are cross-benches for other parties or independents.

The second group of people will be the officials of the council—the chief executive, director of administration, director of finance, committee clerks and other chief officials who may have an interest in the business before the council. The last group of people will be the press and public who are there as observers and take no part in proceedings unless some deputation from the public is asked to make representations on some topic on the agenda.

One point about the council in relation to the committee system should be mentioned. The method by which any committee reaches a decision is determined by the standing orders of the council and the remit of the particular committee. These are laid down by the council and can only be amended or suspended by the council. Thus, as was said at the beginning of this section, the council is supreme in the decision-making process and, although a committee may take a unanimous decision on an issue, it is still open to the council to overturn that decision.

Not all councils are organised along party lines but it may be as well to consider this aspect of council pattern since many are highly political in the party sense of the word. In Scotland, as in England, where parties have representation on a council they are usually organised into party groups on the parliamentary model. This means that they will normally meet before a full council meeting and discuss the council agenda, and members are required to abide by the decisions of the group on pain of suspension or expulsion from the group. This is the "party whip" system and it very often applies to committee meetings as well as full council meetings. Councils with a highly developed party system will often give *de facto* recognition to the system—group rooms, secretarial help, regular meetings between group officials and chief officers, etc. Although party organisation may be regretted by some, it may well help to oil the wheels of decision-making although, of course, making extra demands on a member's time.

Another aspect of the council is the municipal year and meeting cycle. The first is determined by two events—the election in an election year and the annual budget. Since elections are in May, a reconstruction of the leaders of the council and the composition of the committees takes place then. Some councils reconstitute chairman and committee composition each year or every two years irrespective of elections.

The annual budget, however, does not take account of elections. There are specific dates laid down by statute for the submission of budgets by authorities to the Secretary of State for Scotland and these necessarily determine the budget timetable. The local authority financial year has now been brought into line with the central government's financial year—April 1 to March 31. By statute local authorities have to fix their non-domestic rate poundage and community charge before the end of January each year, which means that the decision on the charges to be levied has usually to be made in the preceding November or December. Committees therefore spend much of their time from September to December reviewing the estimates.

The final aspect of council and committee work to be considered is what might be called information flow. This is the manner by which council or committee decisions are communicated to the public and press. Following the Widdicombe committee's interim report in 1985 the Local Government (Access to Information) Act 1985 was enacted to ensure that the public had a right to more information about the workings of their local authorities and more access to their deliberations. Under this Act members of the public and press have a right to attend committee and sub-committee meetings unless a resolution is passed to discuss an item or a series of items in private—normally described as the "B" agenda. Usually the items discussed in private relate to contracts or personal cases.

As to the publication of minutes, again there is a requirement in the 1973 and 1985 Acts to allow public inspection of council and committee minutes and documents. However, some local authorities, before the 1985 Act, already made these documents available in local libraries, council offices, etc. as a matter of practice.

Taking these two aspects together it can be seen that, although a council or committee (or sub-committee) may exclude the press and the public from some (or all) of its proceedings, the minutes of the "private" session can be made available immediately to the public. It is usually the discussion that is confidential and not the decision, and a distinction must be made between the two.

The Committee System

Before the proposals for the reform of the structure of local government were discussed there had been some criticism of the committee system. The committee system at that time was regarded as inefficient and time-consuming with too much time spent on detail and too little on long-term planning and policy decisions.

Although proposals for reform of the committee system were suggested as necessary at the time of reorganisation, in this aspect of local government, as with other aspects, the old conventions have been difficult to change, and therefore it is important to be aware of the traditional committee system.

Local authorities have for a long time had the powers to create committees to discharge their functions. Even the smallest local authorities created committees, albeit that every member of council was on every committee. The large authorities created an often very elaborate system of committees.

The committee system has been underwritten by central government departments through the legislative system by insisting that certain local authority functions are exercised through a committee, e.g. education and planning. These types of committees are known as statutory committees. In recent years, of course, legislation has been drafted to allow more flexibility in terms of statutory committees, with the result that some functions which previously demanded a separate committee (e.g. police) have been amalgamated with other functions (e.g. fire) to create committees perhaps described as protective services.

Apart from statutory committees, local authorities are free to create whatever committees they feel necessary, and committees which are thus created are often described as permissive committees, e.g. recreation, general purposes, personnel, etc.

It is a feature of the committee system that committees spawn sub-committees and sometimes sub-sub-committees. Their size, number and composition are usually determined by the parent committee and they may be temporary or permanent. Sub-committees are frequently used to consider in more detail certain aspects, functions or areas of a council's responsibilities, and since they often wish to consider confidential items e.g. contracts, personal cases, etc. some, or all, of their meetings will be closed to the public. However sub-committees are useful for finding out detailed information from officials about problems or proposals before councillors, or party groups, develop a policy.

The traditional principles underlying the committee system have determined the internal organisation and structure of local authorities. First, services and functions should be clearly identifi-able and usually associated with a particular profession, e.g. finance, education, social work, water supplies, roads, etc. Secondly, for each district service there should be a committee to run it, a chief officer and departmental officials to administer the service. Thus, in summary, we had this form:

one function—one committee—one chief officer—one depart-ment.

This was followed through with a part of a service:

one part of a service—one sub-committee—one section head—one section.

This identification of a committee with a service and a department fitted into the attitude of mind that *policy* and *administration* were quite distinct. Thus the committee made the policy and the department implemented it.

Committees and Departments

Probably the next most important feature of committees, apart from structure, is their size. The number of members will affect the working of the committee in terms of formality/informality, its methods of reaching decisions and the amount of work each member of council has to do. The larger the committee the more formal will its procedures be, also the more difficult will it be to agree and the more committees will the member have to attend. The Paterson report pointed out that the most usual size of a committee, under the old system of local government, was between 30 and 40 per cent of the full council membership. This could mean committees of up to 30 members. Education committees were often very large because of the statutory requirement to co-opt members from religious denominations.

Most of the people who attend committee meetings are elected members, one of whom is the chairperson (or convener). A number of chief officers (or directors) will also be present, including the chief officer most concerned with the committee—the director of education, the director of housing, etc. There will be a committee clerk (the director of administration or his representative), whose responsibility it is to arrange the agenda and circulate all the relevant papers for each item of business. The committee clerk is also responsible for procedural matters and advice about some legal aspects of the committee's work. There will also be present the "finance clerk" (the director of finance or his representative) who is, of course, responsible for giving advice on all aspects of the financial work of the committee.

In addition to the officials mentioned in the preceding paragraph there will be present those other officials who are closely involved in the business of the committee, e.g. chief architect, estates surveyor, etc. These officials, or their representatives, may be present at every meeting of the committee or only on those occasions when advice is required. Some officials may only attend for one item of an agenda.

Some local authorities make it a practice to co-opt certain other non-elected members to committees. These are people who may have a particular expertise or who are representative of some area or group. As mentioned above, under the 1973 Act education authorities are required to co-opt representatives of religious denominations and also must now co-opt members of the teaching profession. Apart from the education committee, the only other committee likely to have co-opted members is the building control committee in the cities, which took over the functions of the old Dean of Guild court where, in fact, the councillors were co-opted to the membership of the court. Under the 1973 Act the number of co-opted members should not exceed one-third of the total numbers of the committee. Proposed legislation following Widdicombe will change the status of co-opted members as will be described later in this chapter.

Another method of gaining expert or representative advice has been devised, mainly by regional councils, since 1975. This is the advisory committee. The council or one of its committees sets up a committee largely of representatives of outside bodies or organisations—the "consumers" of a particular service—to which are added two or three elected members. It is felt that such an advisory body is a good method for members and officials to keep up with the latest developments and to see how the service is being "received" by the users. These advisory committees are mainly in the education and recreational fields.

Corporate Management

In the 1960s central government departments were being restructured and streamlined to promote more efficient administration, and consequently there was pressure on local authorities to change their internal organisational structures. Both the Maud report on the Management of Local Government (1967) and the Wheatley report were critical of the large numbers of committees and the lack of co-ordination. The Wheatley report endorsed the criticism of Maud in these words:

> "What is missing in local government is *unified management* . . . Some organ is needed beside the council itself in which aims can be formulated for the authority as a whole, as well as the means of achieving these aims" (para. 950).

In 1972 the Paterson committee was set up to consider the best type of committee and management structure for the new local authorities. The structure which Paterson recommended brought to local government in Scotland two new concepts, one at committee level and the other at officer level.

At the committee level the Paterson report proposed a new committee called the policy and resources committee, the function of which was to include the responsibility:

> "for identifying and setting out for consideration by the whole council the fundamental objectives which the council should be aiming to achieve . . . it should have a free-ranging remit enabling it to monitor and review the performance of service committees and departments towards the attainment of the Council's objectives" (para. 4.18).

With regard to the composition of the policy and resources committee the report reviewed three options:
(a) composed solely of the majority party—the cabinet-type system;
(b) to have minority party representation on the main committee but have a sub-committee consisting of majority party representation only;
(c) to have a multi-party committee.
However, it did not recommend any particular option, although it did say that:

> "Whatever approach is adopted we stress the need to make effective arrangements for the provision of officer advice to the party groups prior to decisions being taken" (para. 4.27).

The other new aspect which the report brought to internal management was the chief executive and management team. The chief executive was not to have direct responsibility for a department in the traditional sense of the clerk's or treasurer's department but, in the larger authorities, he would have an "executive office." The role of the management team was to:

"act as the focal point for the preparation and presentation to the council, via the policy and resources committee and the service committees, of co-ordinated advice on policies, and major programmes of work" (para. 4.33).

These innovations were intended to sweep away the "excessive departmentalism" which had been seen as restricting decision-making. The type of system proposed by Paterson is usually referred to as corporate management.

Most local authorities in Scotland have made changes in the direction of the Paterson report, although some of these changes may be superficial. To some observers, however, changes in the management structure have only served to tilt the balance towards the officials at the expense of the elected member and the public.

The Widdicombe Report
The Paterson report could, nowadays, be seen as a historical curiosity simply because many of the local authorities have abandoned much of what they adopted from the report. However it serves to give us a foundation upon which to understand the recommendations of the Widdicombe report.

Relations between central and local government had not been good since the mid-1970s when restrictions on local authority finance were first introduced. By the 1980s however that relationship had further declined to, in many cases, direct confrontation. One reason for this was that many urban local authorities had become controlled by younger Labour councillors who had little time for what they saw as the "subservient" attitudes of their predecessors. Many Labour councils simply defied the government's restrictions on finance to the brink of illegality and even past that.

After the 1983 general election the situation got worse and the government became increasingly impatient with what it described as "extremists" in local government. One method of trying to solve the situation was adopted in England—abolition of certain local authorities. In Scotland however the Conservatives were alarmed at the loss of their pride and joy—Edinburgh District Council. For all the above reasons and also for party political advantage the Conservative government in 1984 set up the Widdicombe committee to investigate the "Conduct of Local Government Business".

The terms of reference of the committee were very wide indeed, but the main aspects of business which it was expected to cover included:

- ensuring proper accountability for decision-taking to elected members and to the electorate;
- clarifying the status and role of party groups in decision-taking
- ensuring the proper participation and the accountability of individual elected members;
- examining any problems of propriety which may arise from members' conflicts of interests, particularly where officers of one council serve as councillors of another;
- considering the merits of the development of full-time councillors;
- reviewing the system of co-option of non-elected members;
- studying officers' relationships with elected members and political groups;
- clarifying the limits and conditions governing discretionary spending for political purposes or in relation to bodies set up by local authorities.

The committee issued an interim report in 1985 which resulted in legal restrictions on the use of public money for what the government saw as party political propaganda. This aspect has already been referred to earlier in the chapter. The final report of the committee was published in June 1986.

It is still difficult to assess what the government hoped the Widdicombe committee would do. Some commentators have suggested that the government wanted a "respectable" excuse for further restrictions on the powers of councils and councillors. If this was the motive for the government's action then it must have been sadly disappointed.

The committee concerned itself with the internal workings of councils and ranged its inquiry across England, Wales and Scotland. However its general tenor is that local government institutions were coping well at a time of considerable change. Although the report seemed to regret the increased politicisation of many local authorities it accepted this as a fact of life, much as the Royal Commissions before it had.

The recommendations were, therefore, based on attempting to

strengthen the democratic process albeit by proposals to institute statutory codes, legally enforceable remedies and new or strengthened local government agencies. These were intended to deal with what even the committee accepted, were "limited" abuses.

For Scotland the Widdicombe committee suggested bringing local councillors here more into line with their English colleagues. Scottish councillors should have to declare their intention to act within the law on taking up office. Similarly the Scottish courts should be allowed to disqualify councillors once they had been surcharged not, as at present, on being declared bankrupt after surcharge.

For the British local government system there were many other recommendations with regard to paying councillors, statutory powers for chief executives, the composition and role of policy and executive committees, the abolition of "twin tracking" (see below), increased powers for the local government ombudsman and restrictions on the rights of co-opted members.

Before anything could be done about the report another general election intervened, and it was not until 1989 that the government got round to translating the Widdicombe recommendations into legislation. The Local Government and Housing Bill was published in February 1989 and applies to England, Wales and Scotland. The main provisions which cover Scotland are:

(1) Restrictions on the political activities of senior officials. Staff earning over £13,500 a year will be banned from standing as councillors. This practice has been dubbed "twin-tracking" where officials of one council are councillors on another council. Teachers and the police are exempt from this restriction and the Secretary of State will appoint an arbiter who will consider other exemptions.

(2) Limitation of staff time off from their duties for activities such as trade union conferences.

(3) Co-opted members of committees will lose their voting rights except the religious nominees on education committees.

(4) Rules to ensure political balance on committees.

(5) The adoption of standing orders on certain staffing matters.

(6) Councils will require to appoint a "propriety officer" whose duty would be to report to the council on any contravention of the law by members or staff of the council. This officer has been dubbed the "whistle-blower".

(7) The right to dispose of all the housing stock if councils so wish.

CHAPTER 4

PUBLIC ACCOUNTABILITY

MANY commentators have pointed to the growth of "big government" in recent years and it has been fashionable to talk not only of national bureaucracies but local bureaucracies as well. To many people there is a feeling of frustration when faced with the decisions of a government department or a local authority.

As a reaction to this situation there have been two trends in the political system. First, government itself has responded to demands for more participation in the decision-making process by legislating for participation or redress of grievances. Secondly, people have been organising themselves into groups in order to further some particular local cause or to reverse governmental decisions which they see as harmful to their interests. This chapter is concerned with these aspects of local government.

Community Councils
As with most of local government reform the Wheatley report is the starting point for consideration of many innovations. The report was conscious of the fact that it was recommending larger local government units than had existed before. With fewer local authorities it was obvious that there would be fewer elected members. There could now be a wider gap between the electors and the elected. This possibility conflicted with the balance, which the Wheatley commission wanted to keep, between democracy and efficiency.

During the course of its investigations the commission sponsored a community survey. The findings of this survey were to indicate to the commission the difficulties to be experienced in defining "a local community". Nevertheless the commission felt it necessary to recommend the setting up of community councils. The characteristics of these new bodies were set out in the report and these were to be: "a broadly-based unit, with an official standing, to which the local community as a whole can give allegiance and through which it can speak and act" (para. 848).

Under the 1973 Act district and islands authorities were given the responsibility for submitting schemes for community councils and these were to be submitted by May 1976. Submissions of these schemes were required to provide for a number of items which the local authority should consider when it eventually set up community councils. These items included:

(a) description of the areas selected and their boundaries;
(b) proposed composition indicating which proportions were to be elected or appointed;
(c) methods of election and appointment;
(d) some constitutional requirements including term of office of members, minimum number of meetings, etc;
(e) proposals regarding finance;
(f) proposals regarding information procedures.

Initially over 1300 were proposed in Scotland. Thus, if all the places were filled, there would be 12 times as many directly elected community councillors as there are district and island councillors. Altogether there was some cynicism at first about community councils, partly because they were to have no statutory responsibilities and no statutory methods of raising money (rating) but there was, at first, a reasonable response to the innovation.

This response was mainly from those people willing to serve on community councils. A research survey of the first elections to community councils showed that 35 per cent of all community councillors were elected at contested elections, although this indicates that 65 per cent were returned unopposed. Turnout, the survey showed, varied considerably from area to area but the average was just over 16 per cent of registered voters. Considerable differences occurred on turnout depending on the method used. Ballot by public meeting showed a 7 per cent turnout whereas postal ballots showed a response of 54 per cent.

It would seem that despite the slow start community councils, particularly in the old small burgh and rural parts of Scotland, have played an effective part in involving local people in the decision-making process of local government. Their value in the larger urban areas however may be doubted. The creation of community councils in these areas seems to be patchy. Very often the interest lies in middle-class areas, leaving large council house estates (perhaps the areas most in need of pressurising local authorities) without community councils. The types of issues which community councils take up are essentially local issues mainly concerned with planning and licensing. Their mode of operation is to gather the views of the local people on a particular proposal and channel these views to the local elected representatives and, if necessary, lobby the council or one of its committees.

Part of the problem, particularly in urban areas, is the existence of a number of local voluntary organisations which were in existence before community councils were set up. In this situation the local community council may have to compete for influence. Also, in terms of active personnel, there might be overlapping. It would seem, therefore, that community councils are more influential where there are no, or only weak, local voluntary organisations with which to compete.

School Councils

Unlike community councils, school councils were not recommended by the Wheatley commission. Apart from expressing concern about the possible size of the new education authorities the Wheatley commission, inexplicably, did not even suggest any solution to the possible "remoteness" which these larger education authorities might create.

Section 125 of the Local Government (Scotland) Act 1973 empowered local education authorities to set up school and college councils "to discharge . . . such of the functions of management and supervision of educational establishments . . . as the authority shall determine". In other words it was entirely up to the local authority to determine what, if any, functions were the responsibility of these councils. Unlike community councils there was no guidance from central government about the functions or composition of school or college councils.

The section in the Act did not say how the composition of a school council should be made up, except to say that there should be "due representation of the parents" and "at least one person interested in the promotion of religious education". In addition the Act allowed for the representation of teaching and other staff employed in the school. For colleges the composition should be made up to include "due representation of persons concerned or engaged in crafts, industries, commerce or other employments in the locality" together with representation from local interests.

As previously mentioned, the Act made no reference to the functions of school and college councils. The consequence of this was that each education authority produced its own scheme. School councils were normally based on the catchment area of a secondary school with its feeder primaries although this could differ in some areas.

The functions of school councils also differed from area to area. Many had an "attendance" responsibility. This meant that a sub-committee was charged, in conjunction with the attendance officer, with finding reasons, from pupils, teachers and parents, for a particular pupil's attendance record. Most school councils had responsibility for community use of school premises outside school hours and also had some say about such items as school uniforms, school meals, extra-curricular activities, etc.

There were, however, two controversial areas where there was a clash between community involvement and professional activities. These were staff appointments and the school curriculum. Some education authorities agreed that since parents and the community had an interest in the type of staff who teach their children, there should be a parental and/or community representative present when teachers were being interviewed for a post. In some areas this was implemented only when posts like assistant head teacher were being filled. Teachers' unions have never liked this particular provision since, they argue, only a professional (i.e. the directorate) can judge the value of another professional.

Similarly with the curriculum school councils did not have the power to alter the school curriculum as decided by the head teacher and his staff. No doubt many school council representatives, from time to time, passed judgment on the school curriculum and many teachers were prepared to listen to the views of parents and others in this respect. However, the teachers' unions were always opposed to any interference in areas, like the curriculum, which they regarded as a professional matter.

School Boards

The above description of school councils serves two purposes. First, it provides us with a historical view of a system which was new in 1975 and which, on the whole, seemed to work reasonably well. Secondly, it provides us with a measuring rod to set against the new system which the School Boards (Scotland) Act 1988 brings into existence in 1989.

In 1987 the Conservative government issued a consultative document on school management. It was the Scottish dimension of proposals which had been implemented in England reforming the system of school governors. Both sets of proposals were based on the theory that the parents' charter proposals of 1981 should be taken a step further and that parents should be given more power over their children's education than was provided for in the existing school management system.

Whatever positive side there was to the new proposals, there were some critics who saw a negative and sinister side to them. Giving more power to school boards was bound to take away powers from education authorities unless, of course, more powers were to be given to education authorities. Giving more power to education authorities could only be done by taking away powers from the Scottish Education Department. This latter scenario would not happen and thus these critics argued that this was a further erosion of local authority powers.

After receiving considerable response to their initial proposals the government issued another set of proposals which made some concessions to the concerns expressed. On the basis of these new proposals the government went ahead to legislate for them in the School Boards (Scotland) Act 1988.

In essence the system to be established abolishes school councils and replaces these with a school board for every primary, secondary and special school regardless of size, with the following features:

(1) The boards will be composed of a majority of parents (up to seven) elected from the parents; up to three staff members chosen by their colleagues although these need not all be teachers; up to three co-opted members chosen by the board and who could be parents, staff or local representatives. Since the parents hold the majority of places it is likely that the co-opted members will at least be sympathetic to the elected parents.

(2) The powers of school boards will be delegated to them by the local education authority.

(3) School boards will not be allowed to interfere in professional issues rightly the responsibility of teachers but they will be able to "give advice forcibly", in the government's words, since they can claim that they represent the views of the parents and the local community.

(4) School boards will have a role in appointing senior staff and will be able to make representation to the local education authority on the appointment of other staff.

As a first step to the setting up of school boards and in an attempt to assess the practical implications of the proposals, local authorities were asked to become "guinea pigs" for the new system. Only Dumfries and Galloway Regional Council volunteered for the experiment and school boards were set up there in the academic year 1988–89, although the legislation is not due to be implemented generally until 1989–90.

Although the government had consistently said in the early stages of the legislation that it was not going to give the new school boards powers to "opt out", ministerial statements have changed and, at the time of writing, legislation is being prepared to allow schools in Scotland to "opt out" with certain safeguards for small and special schools. "Opting out" will not make these schools private schools but they will be directly financed by the Scottish Education Department and local education authority control will be limited to ensuring adequate provision in their area.

Voluntary Organisations

The 1960s saw an increase in the number of groups concerned with specific local problems. The main stimulus for this was the number of planning decisions made by local authorities particularly with regard to redevelopment schemes and motorway construction. These decisions seemed not to have taken account of local interests and needs. It was for this reason that the Skeffington report, *People and Planning*, was published, and subsequent legislation has made it incumbent on local authorities to publicise their planning decisions and to consult with local interests.

It was not just in the planning field that pressure groups or interest groups developed. Protests about living conditions in new mass housing schemes of high storey flats, about lack of any nursery facilities, about lack of recreational facilities, created a sort of "issue politics" at the grass roots, often concerned with the quality of the environment. Added to this in recent years is a growing number of groups concerned with conservation and with housing rehabilitation and dampness.

Local authorities have had to take more notice of these groups than central government simply because of the decisions which these local authorities have had to take in the fields of planning, housing, education, etc. Very often, of course, councils and councillors have seen these pressure and interest groups as politically motivated but this type of development is not peculiar to Britain. We have had pressure and interest group politics at national level for many years but the response at local level is almost certainly due to the bureaucratisation of local government. Since large local authorities are unlikely to disappear it would seem that these issue groups are here to stay, although they have very often amalgamated into powerful community organisations which compete, as noted earlier, with community councils.

The role and future of voluntary community organisations at local level is probably dependent on availability of money. Some of these organisations, unlike community councils, have been powerful enough to extract money from regional and district authorities and also from the European Community. However, as local authorities cut back on expenditure this, in turn, reduces the "matching funds" which the European Community requires when it gives grants.

Local authorities have tried to cope with the problems of greater citizen participation by the appointment of various types of community social workers. The manifestation of community education programmes in Scotland is a direct result of the realisation by local authorities of the need to cater for the needs and listen to the views of groups of people with particular needs or problems.

There seems little doubt, therefore, that despite the success or otherwise of community councils, voluntary organisations at the local level who take up local issues will stay as part of the local government scene. Many local authorities have tried to cater for this, but whether they will continue to allocate sometimes scarce resources remains to be seen.

Local Government Ombudsman

Local groups trying to solve local problems in a collective way may be one thing, but when individuals have a personal grievance what machinery can redress this? In the 1960s central government came to realise that the complexities of its own procedures often caused people to suffer unnecessarily. There was pressure, led by MPs, to create some system which would sit in judgment on the actions of "faceless" civil servants. It was out of this pressure that the Parliamentary Commissioner for Administration—"the Ombudsman"—was created.

It is not surprising to find that the Wheatley report discussed briefly the arguments for and against the setting up of a local government system for redress of grievances. No recommendation was made but the Local Government (Scotland) Act 1975 (not the 1973 Act) set up the office of Commissioner for Local Administration in Scotland. The aim of this machinery was to give members of the public who felt that they had been the victim of maladministration by any local authority (or joint board) the same right to have their complaints independently scrutinised as they have through the Parliamentary Commissioner for Administration.

The Commissioner for Local Administration in Scotland is appointed by the Secretary of State for Scotland in consultation with the local authorities. He has two functions laid down by statute: first, to publish an annual report on the complaints investigated each year and the outcome of these investigations; secondly, to keep under review the machinery for investigating complaints and recommending any necessary changes.

The authorities whose activities are subject to investigation are the following:

- regional, district and islands authorities;
- committees, joint committees or boards with members appointed by local authorities;
- river purification boards.

Where a local authority delegates its powers to a particular body the actions of such bodies are liable to investigation also.

The matters which are subject to investigation are any complaint made by or on behalf of a member of the public who claims to have sustained injustice consequent upon action (or non-action) by an authority. Certain rules however are laid down concerning the procedure for such complaints. Under the 1975 Act the complaint had to be channelled through a local councillor, but the Local Government Act 1988 now allows the complainant to go directly to the Commissioner. Further, the complaint must be within 12 months of the matter, unless the Commissioner considers that it is reasonable to entertain a later complaint; the complaint must not be a matter for any court or tribunal; the complaint must be an individual complaint and not a collective complaint common to a number of people.

There is provision in the legislation for the Commissioner not to investigate the complaint if he thinks there are no grounds for this; however he must give reasons for so deciding. If a complaint has been investigated then he must report his findings and recommendations to the parties concerned. One difficulty which has been criticised is that although the Commissioner may recommend that the complaint be remedied, there is no legal obligation on the local authority so to do. However it is up to the councillors, not the council officials, to decide what action, if any, should be taken.

The undernoted statistics give some indication of the scale and nature of the complaints investigated by the Commissioner in 1987–88:

Number of cases referred	662
Number of cases investigated	62

Nature of those investigated:

Housing	57.8%
Planning	15.2%
Land and property	9.5%
Education	2.1%
Miscellaneous	15.4%

Some explanation is needed of the above statistics. First, the apparently small number of cases investigated compared to the number referred. There are a variety of reasons for this, mostly concerned with there being no basis for the complaint; the complaint being a collective complaint rather than an individual one; the complaint having been remedied before the Commissioner did his preliminary investigation; the complaint not being properly processed through a councillor. Of the numbers investigated in 1987–88, just under half found in favour of the complainant but there is no record as to the councils' response to remedying the respective complaints.

CHAPTER 5

EXPENDITURE

LOCAL government finance has always been controversial. Since the nineteenth century local authorities have had to look to central government to finance some of the local services. After the Second World War it was the policy of all governments to lay down standards for services, and they had to supply taxpayers' money to ensure that local authorities maintained these standards.

In this sense local authorities have become more dependent on central government and the consequence of this has been that central government has used local authority expenditure as one of a number of economic weapons in pursuit of whatever is the current financial philosophy. This has meant that local authorities have had to change their financial procedures to cope with these new circumstances.

Much of this chapter is taken up with describing the traditional procedures used by local authorities, the methods by which central government has attempted to control local authority expenditure and the reactions by local authorities to these controls.

Financial Accounts

There is hardly any need to stress the importance of local government finance. Indeed it was argued at the time when the Royal Commissions were set up in 1966 that it was a grave omission that they should not investigate finance. It was argued also that, if anything was wrong with local government, it was because of the finance available, or not available, to the local authorities and therefore looking at structure was a cosmetic job where the root cause of the problems of local government was money.

This section will concern itself with the current practice with regard to financial procedures. By the nature of it, these procedures are complex and at times detailed, but have been built up over many years. Changes are difficult to make, even where the newer ideas of corporate management have been implemented.

Many of the procedures which local authorities adopt for expenditure are forced upon them by central government. For instance, although it is usual practice in terms of expenditure to keep separate capital and revenue accounts, over the last few years central government has insisted that the local authorities keep separate housing accounts—both capital and revenue. Each of these accounts will be explained in the next few paragraphs.

Leaving aside the peculiar nature of housing accounts, "capital" and "revenue" have a particular meaning in local government. Broadly speaking, expenditure of a capital nature covers items which have a lasting value, although the value may diminish (depreciate) in time. The largest group of items of this nature would be the "bricks and mortar" of the authority—schools, halls, sports centres, roads, sewers, together with the necessary land.

However, this definition of capital leaves a lot of room for interpretation. It is easy to assume that large items are capital items, but there are many small items which also have lasting value—yet one authority may put these under "revenue" and another authority may put them under "capital".

Examples of these would include cars and vans, microcomputers and maintenance equipment. Indeed it is because there are considerable "grey areas" between capital and revenue items that some local authorities have been able to exercise "creative accountancy", which will be explained later.

Essentially revenue items are the non-permanent or consumable elements of the authority's expenditure, and include wages and salaries, heating and lighting, insurance, normal property and maintenance costs, supplies (like cleaning materials, food, etc.) and, surprisingly, non-domestic rates.

This division into capital and revenue is not just an academic distinction—it is vitally important in determining how such expenditure is to be financed. Because it has the power to borrow money for capital items, a local authority can spread the cost of these items over the assumed life of the asset, thus reducing the immediate impact on expenditure. In contrast, it meets the cost of revenue expenditure in the year in which it was incurred and cannot borrow in the long term to meet this expenditure although, once again, in recent years authorities have got round this by covenant schemes which will also be explained later.

In practice local authorities keep a number of different accounts, partly because of legislation, e.g. housing accounts, and partly because of accounting practice, e.g. general services and departmental accounts. However all local authorities must have a general fund and a consolidated loans fund.

Housing Accounts

Although this chapter is concerned primarily with expenditure, nevertheless this may be a good place to consider the special nature of housing accounts—both expenditure and income. As noted previously those local authorities who have housing responsibilities (districts and islands) are obliged to keep these accounts separate. It is not possible to transfer income or expenditure between housing and general services accounts in the same manner that transfers can be made between general services accounts.

Let us take housing capital expenditure first. The main expenditure in this account is on the building of new houses, the rehabilitation of older houses and capital maintenance and repair, i.e. repairs, like new roofs, which are needed to the structure of the building. As indicated in Chapter 2, there has been a decline in new council house building, partially because of the complicated manner in which the government has insisted that money for new building should be raised.

On the income side of the housing capital account is money borrowed, which is subject to government limits and controls, and receipts from the sale of council houses. In the early 1980s many Labour authorities were loth to sell council houses and found excuses for dragging their feet. The government responded by increasing the discount to sitting tenants, thereby increasing the potential sales, and then linking sales receipts to new building. The irony of the present situation is that the more the council sells its houses the more money it has to build new ones and these same Labour councils are now actively, if reluctantly, selling houses.

The housing revenue account (HRA) has been the main area for change and controversy in the last few years. Included under the heading of HRA expenditure is repayment of capital, interest charges, regular repair and maintenance, management, community charge, and loss of rent. Each of these expenditure heads has to be explained.

Capital repayment and interest charges are in historic terms which means, since capital borrowing for houses is usually on a 60 year term, that the council is still repaying capital and interest on houses which it has sold. Council house building only started in earnest in the 1920s. As indicated earlier, maintenance costs have risen in recent years, once again because of sales. It tends to be the better maintained houses in better areas that get sold thus leaving older and poorer houses which require more maintenance. Because of the difficulty of finding money for maintenance, the "creative accountancy" schemes like covenants (which will be explained in Chapter 6) were often used for this purpose.

It may seem surprising that councils are required to pay a proportion of the community charge for property since it is a charge on people. However legislation demands that "void" houses—those presently with no tenants—are assumed to have one tenant and, as landlord, the council is obliged to pay a proportion of the charge for this notional tenant. Finally, it is obvious that as houses are sold there will be a loss of rent and this has to be taken account of in expenditure. Also there will be loss of rent where tenants fail to pay and the amount has to be written off. In this respect many factors contribute to this loss. Obviously as rents rise there will be more difficulties in paying rent. Some local authorities have blamed the government's housing benefit scheme, since it is so complicated that many previous recipients are not claiming and, therefore, have less income to pay rent.

Included under the heading of HRA income is rents, revenue fund income, the housing support grant and agency fees. Each of these has to be explained. Rents now constitute 80 per cent of income on HRA, a figure which has risen steadily throughout the 1980s because of the government's policy of trying to make housing self-financing. Revenue fund income was previously designated the rate fund contribution until the introduction of the community charge. Most local authorities transfer an amount from their general services revenue account to the HRA, principally to keep rents down. Once again the government, in recent years, has devised methods to try to limit or reduce this amount.

The housing support grant was the government's contribution to housing which paralleled the rate (now revenue) support grant. This too has been steadily reduced and, in 1988, only 33 of the 56 housing authorities qualified for this grant—almost 50 per cent of this went to Glasgow. Dundee and Edinburgh did not qualify.

Many local authorities act as agents for service providers. They may, for instance, install and maintain gas or electric heating systems and charge the respective company a fee for this service.

Budgetary Procedures

Although some local authorities took the opportunity, at local government reform, to implement new budgetary procedures, it must be admitted that few local authorities changed their procedures in any radical way. This is not to say that traditional approaches have been retained, but such changes as have taken place have been in response to outside, mainly central government, pressures rather than any desire from within the authorities to change procedures. Some tried the new systems but reverted to the old practices.

Financial procedures in a local authority inevitably centre round the annual budget. Whatever procedures, new or old, are adopted by a local authority, there is a statutory requirement to fix the non-domestic rate and the community charge during the month of

January. The traditional method of proceeding with an annual budget was for each department of the authority to calculate its costs for its ongoing activities—in other words, to assume the service would continue at the same pace as in the previous year. Added to this would be the costs incurred in creating new services or developing or expanding existing services.

These departmental estimates would then be submitted to the appropriate committee for their approval or amendment. The estimates would then go from the service committees to the treasurer, who would aggregate the various estimates, add amounts for inflation and contingencies, deduct estimated revenue grants and then calculate the rate poundage, i.e. the amount per pound necessary to meet the estimated expenditure. These provisional estimates would then go to the finance committee, who would review the aggregate amounts and, if they regarded the amounts as too high, refer all or some of the departmental estimates back to the service committees.

In recent years this traditional budgeting system has undergone considerable changes. These changes have been the result of the implementation of corporate management, and, more importantly, the imposition of strict spending guidelines by central government. The traditional system has had to take account of the implementation of cash limits by central government. This method of controlling local authority expenditure (capital and revenue) has forced local authorities to adopt a system which, effectively, turns the traditional system on its head.

As explained above, the traditional procedure was for service committees to calculate their own estimates and process these through the finance committee (or sub-committee). The total estimates (normally trimmed by the finance committee) were simply all the service committee estimates added up. Cash limits, however, entail the central government and/or the finance (or policy) committee deciding beforehand what the total expenditure should be and then indicating to the service committee their share of this total. The committee then have discretion as to how they spend their share. Additional expenditure required later would have to get approval from the policy committee.

The cash limit system was imposed by central government as a response to the economic difficulties of the mid-1970s and has been tightened under the financial controls of the present Conservative government. Many local authorities have chosen to adopt this system in any event because it strengthens the corporate management process and allows local authorities to consider resource allocation. However, it would be wrong to suggest that cash limits have resulted in widespread discussion of the objectives of local authorities or the objectives of particular local government services.

Financial Control

The calculation of estimates and the control of expenditure is largely the task of the director of finance and the finance department. By its very nature the finance department will involve a great deal of specialist knowledge and work. Finance departments, nevertheless, will vary from authority to authority but, generally speaking, will be involved in the following tasks:

- all matters pertaining to estimates;
- control of expenditure;
- internal and external audit;
- payment of accounts and collection of income;
- review of charges;
- investment of funds;
- banking and insurance arrangements;
- borrowing;
- pay control.

As far as internal audit is concerned, the Chartered Institute of Public Finance and Accountancy (CIPFA) have attempted to lay down standard principles and practices which suggest that the objective of internal audit should be:

(1) a system of control;
(2) the improvement and continuous review of controls and procedures;
(3) continuous examination to eliminate fraud, waste, and irregular expenditure; and
(4) monitoring the use of resources.

As can be seen, internal audit has become a wider exercise than mere financial control, and many observers have felt that this function should be transferred from the director of finance's department to the chief executive's office, particularly that part of internal audit dealing with performance review. However, there are many disadvantages to this move—not least that it might weaken the ability of the finance department to keep a continuous check on financial matters.

The Local Government (Scotland) Act 1973 lays down the functions of the Commission for Local Authority Accounts in Scotland—the Accounts Commission. Under section 97 (2) of that Act these functions include: (a) securing the audit of all accounts of local authorities; (b) advising the Secretary of State on any matter relating to the accounting of local authorities which he may refer to them for advice. This form of external audit was an innovation for local authorities and has created some criticism about interference in local authority decision-making. The reason for this criticism is the method by which the Accounts Commission carries out its remit.

The Controller of Audit, who is the chief official, issues particular reports on his observations of local authority accounts. He can issue special "malpractices" reports under the 1973 Act (see also Chapter 3, under Councillors). There is a statutory requirement by the Commission to present an annual report to Parliament. The views in this annual report are usually based on specific reports by auditors about general practices (or problems of procedure) adopted by individual local authorities.

The individual auditor's reports to local authorities contain advice about the organisation of an authority's financial affairs. Some local authorities see this as widening the scope of audit into the efficiency field and involving political judgments which auditors should not be involved in. The Commission claims that it (and the various auditors) are simply carrying out the will of Parliament as expressed in legislation.

Recent reports by the Accounts Commission and the Controller of Audit have been critical of some "creative accountancy" practices of local authorities. This is seen as both passing on debt to future generations particularly on revenue accounts and also infusing an element of unpredictability into financial procedures. Both of these consequences are felt to be inimical to good accountancy procedures.

The Local Government Act 1988 extended the powers of the Accounts Commission. This legislation lays a duty on the Commission to undertake studies of local authorities with the aim of getting better "value for money". However the Act does not allow the Commission to take into account the actions of central government on local authority services. The Commission feels this is a regrettable omission from the Act, especially since it was included in the legislation for England and Wales.

Central Government Controls

As indicated earlier, all governments over the last two decades have been pursuing restraint on public expenditure. Local authorities' expenditure amounts to almost a third of total public expenditure and, therefore, what local authorities do is important to government policies.

The machinery for what has been called "macro-economic

management" has become very sophisticated in recent years. The most general control which the government has is the Public Expenditure Survey. This sets out annually proposals for future expenditure in the short and medium terms but it is not mandatory on local authorities. The survey simply indicates to the local authorities what the government's priorities are over a period of two or three years. It does, however, give the authorities a clue about the possible nature of the other controls wielded by government.

The second control which the government uses is that over capital investment. This is sometimes referred to as capital allocation and it has two features. First, it can apply to a service, e.g. education or housing, where the government indicates the maximum total amount it expects all local authorities to spend on capital projects within the particular service. Secondly, as far as individual local authorities are concerned, each is given a maximum amount of capital allocation. This individual capital allocation is not just the amount of money which the local authority is likely to *borrow* but is the *total amount it is allowed to spend*. To the central government the *sources* of capital finance (borrowing, grants or out of revenue) are immaterial since the central government is here concerned with capital investment and balancing this between the public and private sectors of the economy.

Another method of control of capital expenditure is loan sanction. For each individual project above an amount laid down from time to time by the central government, a local authority has to get "section 94 consent" (consent of the Secretary of State under section 94 of the 1973 Act). Here the central government is saying to the local authority that it is allowing the local authority to spend its own money on a particular project.

Of course the government has other methods of controlling capital expenditure by local authorities. About a third of all capital borrowed by local authorities is borrowed from the Public Works Loan Board. The board gets its funds directly from the government (authorised by Parliament) and therefore it is possible for the government to limit the amount available to the board, thus restricting the local authorities' sources of borrowing. The government can also restrict the quota which local authorities are allowed to borrow from the board. This quota varies according to need and total outstanding debt. Borrowing from the board is discussed further in Chapter 6.

Through the Bank of England the central government can influence the banks' lending rates, and thus whatever sources local authorities have for borrowing money the market rate can be influenced by government. The level of the rate of interest is a major consideration to a local authority about to borrow for capital projects, since the interest paid is financed out of the revenue account. By increasing interest rates, therefore, the central government indirectly deters any local authorities from borrowing.

The government also controls the revenue expenditure of local authorities but since this is mainly done indirectly by restricting the authorities' income from grants, charges and non-domestic rating, these will be dealt with in the following chapter on sources of finance.

CHAPTER 6

SOURCES OF FINANCE

THE other side of the book-keeping exercise from expenditure is obviously income. Local authority income derives from many sources nowadays but, like expenditure, is broken up into capital and revenue income. Although sources of capital have not changed much in recent years the sources of revenue income are undergoing a major change which has had considerable political repercussions. We shall deal with capital first because it is the easier to understand and is organised on a longer-term basis than revenue income.

Sources of Capital

Local authorities mostly borrow money for capital projects and items. The 1973 Act provides the main powers for local authorities to borrow money. Under this Act they may raise money in a number of ways—mortgages, stock, annuity certificates, bonds, bills or other means approved by the Secretary of State, and they also have powers to raise money outside the United Kingdom. In practice, however, borrowing money is very strictly controlled by central government as indicated in the previous chapter.

Of the sources of capital finance mentioned above, the largest proportion is borrowed from the Public Works Loan Board. The Public Works Loan Board lends money to local authorities and other public agencies. The board is financed by government loans and the rate of interest is prescribed by the Treasury. There is little need to go into the rather complicated procedures used by the board to lend money to local authorities.

Two aspects of the board are important, however. First, local authorities can only borrow so much from the Public Works Loan Board—"the quota", which is equal to a proportion of the local authorities' outstanding debt or annual capital payments. This quota can be varied by the Treasury, depending on the government's financial policies. In addition, the government could deter the local authorities from borrowing from the Public Works Loan Board—thus forcing them into the market. Secondly, since the rate of interest is ultimately controlled by the government, again the government can control the level of local authority borrowing from the Public Works Loan Board.

Nevertheless, there are some advantages in borrowing from this source. Principally, the Public Works Loan Board can be used where other sources of borrowing may be difficult for a local authority, and secondly, the borrowing arrangements are a little more flexible than in the open market. The Public Works Loan Board can also act as a lender of last resort outwith the quota mentioned above—but at a cost.

As mentioned above, local authorities are now allowed to borrow money from sources outside the UK, but this is very strictly controlled by the Treasury and the Bank of England. In recent years this has mainly meant the institutions of the European Community. For instance, loans are available for the following categories of expenditure:
(a) creation of employment in areas of declining industries;
(b) industrial estates and the restoration of derelict land; and
(c) certain specific projects in under-developed regions.

In addition to borrowing for capital projects, both the UK government and the EC will give grants to local authorities for specific projects. The trend in recent years, by the government, has been to provide grants in conjunction with other public agencies, or to channel capital finance through specific agencies. For instance, the Glasgow Eastern Area Renewal (GEAR) project received grants from the Scottish Development Department and the Scottish Development Agency. Again, the EC will give grants for specific projects in agriculture, fishing, retraining, job creation and job maintenance schemes.

The controls which central government has exercised over local authority capital expenditure have varied over the years. The current procedure is that local authorities submit a five-year capital programme to central government. Central government then informs local authorities of their capital allocation—this is the maximum amount which a local authority will be allowed to spend in the next financial year. Within this allocation there are limits to capital spending set for specific services. For example, central government has severely restricted local authority capital spending on recreational facilities in recent years. It must be stressed that capital allocation is not money which the central government gives to local authorities (that would be a grant)—it is the amount local authorities are allowed to spend, no matter how they get that money.

As restrictions on capital expenditure tightened in the early 1980s, particularly in housing, many local authorities tried to find loopholes in the law. This became known as "creative accountancy". It has to be pointed out here that capital spending restrictions were not subject to the same financial penalties as revenue spending restrictions simply because sources of borrowing were not directly controlled by central government.

One method of getting round capital allocations was for local authorities to lease capital items rather than borrow money for them. A variation of this was for local authorities to sell a capital item and then "lease-back". Thus buildings, land or equipment could be sold off, the money used for capital projects and the item leased back from the buyer. The consequence of this, however, was that the leasing payments had to come out of revenue accounts. The government closed this loophole and since March 1987 new lease-back arrangements have not been allowed.

Another method of getting round the restrictions was for local authorities to raise money by "covenant". Basically this meant that local authorities borrowed money from, mainly overseas, banks on a medium term loan at rates of interest higher than the market rate. These loans would be for a specific purpose, often housing, and the capital item would serve as collateral for the loan. The end result of this was to defer payment of the loan over a long period of time and add to revenue expenditure for a long time into the future.

Once again the government acted to close this loophole. Local authorities who financed capital by covenant now find that, although they may have money to spend in the short term, the government reduces their capital allocation in the long term. Over a period of time, therefore, their average capital expenditure has to match what it would have been if the covenants had not been taken out.

It would be wrong to complete an explanation about capital finance without mentioning that new capital borrowing does not occupy a large amount of a finance department's time. Most of the work is concerned with servicing ongoing loans. This can involve the re-financing of existing loans and the management of long-term and temporary borrowing. New capital expenditure amounts to less than a fifth of existing debt.

Sources of Revenue

Turning now to revenue income, this requires some detailed explanation. Local authorities derive their income from three general sources—the community charge (added to which is a water charge), non-domestic rates and the revenue support grant. In addition specific services like social work, recreation, education, etc. generate income from charges for all or part of the service. These charges, however, are designated to the specific service and deducted from the gross expenditure for that service (department).

The total net expenditure for the local authority, i.e. the sum of each department's net expenditure, is met from the community charge, non-domestic rates and revenue support grant.

Under the Abolition of Domestic Rates Etc. (Scotland) Act 1987 domestic rates were abolished in 1989 and replaced by the community charge. Non-domestic rates will remain in the meantime but will be replaced by a unified business rate sometime in the early 1990s. The community charge will be explained in more detail in the next section.

The 1987 Act also changed the system for non-domestic ratepayers. The government intends to introduce a unified business rate which will be levied uniformly throughout Scotland, England and Wales. This proposal is causing some controversy. Scottish property was revalued in 1985 but the last revaluation in England and Wales was 1973. It follows from this that business property in Scotland has a higher assessment rate. The introduction of a British-wide standard rate would, obviously, disadvantage Scottish business. The various business organisations in Scotland have been lobbying hard to persuade the government to have a separate Scottish business rate. In the meantime, pending legislation, non-domestic ratepayers in Scotland will have their rates pegged to the rate of inflation.

The third source of local authority income is the revenue (previously rate) support grant which pays for just over half of aggregate local authority net spending in Scotland, although regions and islands get almost 90 per cent of this because of their educational responsibilities. The calculation of the RSG is complicated and has changed significantly in the last few years.

The global amount of revenue support grant is determined by the government in accordance with the estimates of relevant expenditure by the local authorities. What is "relevant expenditure" is defined by legislation, but includes most of the local authority services except those which receive a specific grant like the police, urban aid or housing.

However, instead of distributing the RSG on a simple headcount basis, a number of factors are taken into account. Part of the calculation takes into account the particular needs of an area. For example, a local authority which has more than the (Scottish) average of school children or old people per head of population will have to devote more of its resources to these groups. Therefore, these groups are "weighted" in the calculation.

As mentioned previously, housing finance is kept separate from other (general services) finance. The system of distribution of support for housing (the housing support grant) is also very complex, but is intended to take account of a number of housing factors, e.g. amount spent on maintenance, level of rents, loan charges, etc., in much the same way as the revenue support grant takes account of general factors in spending.

In addition to the above grants, local authorities can receive specific grants. Like capital grants both central government and other public agencies can give revenue grants. Examples of these are the specific recurrent grants which central government gives for police services and urban aid. Other public agencies, like the Arts Council, the Sports Council and the Countryside Commission, are empowered to give grants for a specific service or project.

The Community Charge

The origins of the community charge lie back in the 1960s. Concern about the level of local authority spending was one element in the setting up of the two Royal Commissions of 1966–69. Both of these commissions, however, excluded a review of local government finance. The government of the day felt that the time to consider finance was after the commissions had reported.

In 1971 the Conservative government issued a green paper, *The Future Shape of Local Government Finance*, in which it set out a number of advantages and disadvantages of a number of alternatives to replace the rating system. Although there was considerable discussion at the time, no further action was taken. After local government reform in 1973–74 there was a considerable rise in the level of rates, sparking off much criticism and protest which the newspapers of the day described as a "ratepayers' revolt". The two main political parties were forced to take account of this in the general elections of 1974. The Conservatives pledged that they would do away with the system and the newly returned Labour government set up an inquiry—the Layfield committee.

The Layfield report, published in 1976, was a very exhaustive study of local government finance and still remains a valuable source of statistics for those interested in the subject. The recommendations, however, are of little value now, although it is worth noting that the committee suggested that local income tax should be explored as a *supplement* to local rating and that valuation of property should shift from rental values to capital values.

As with the 1971 green paper, nothing was done about the Layfield proposals until the Conservative government issued another green paper in 1981, *Alternatives to Domestic Rates*. The message of this document was that there was no viable alternative to the rating system although a variety of supplements could be made to work. By 1983 it seemed that the rating system devised in the nineteenth century was going to remain stubbornly durable.

However events were to bring the issue to crisis point. One of the main criticisms of the rating system was that there were not enough revaluations of property to keep pace with inflation. Valuations were supposed to take place every five years but because of their unpopularity all governments had found excuses for delay or postponement. Scotland was due to have a revaluation in 1985 (the previous revaluation had been 1977) and England and Wales had not had a revaluation since 1973.

Inevitably after long periods between revaluations rental values leapt considerably (up to three times in 1985) and ratepayers became alarmed. The Conservative government responded to this alarm by announcing it would carry out its election pledge (of 1979) to abolish domestic rating. The problem was what to replace it with? To most people's surprise they proposed to replace domestic rates with a poll tax, a flat rate tax on adults, which was to be renamed a community charge. This type of tax had never been seriously considered by the parade of inquiries and green papers since the 1970s. Indeed the government itself had dismissed the idea in 1983.

Nevertheless in 1986 the government's proposals were published in a document *Paying for Local Government*. There was to be legislation for the new tax first in Scotland and then, eventually, in England and Wales. In pursuance of these proposals the Abolition of Domestic Rates Etc. (Scotland) Act 1987 was passed just before the 1987 general election.

From April 1989 in Scotland domestic rates were abolished and replaced by a community charge. In effect there is not one charge but three. The personal charge is a flat rate charge levied on all adults within an area. A standard charge is levied on the owner or the tenants of second and/or holiday homes. Its level could be up to twice the personal charge. Finally there is a collective charge applicable to the owner of premises where there is a high turnover of tenants. The old water rate has also been replaced by a water charge which is added to the community charge.

A rebate system exists for certain categories of adults. These rebates are based on income and savings and are therefore not easy to classify. However the maximum rebate on the community charge is 80 per cent while there is no rebate on the water charge. Social security benefits have been brought into line but they are based on a national average rate of community charge and so people with the same income and savings pay different charges depending on where they live.

These proposals have caused considerable controversy. Although the government found it relatively easy to pass the Scottish legislation it had difficulties in getting its legislation for England and Wales through, particularly in the House of Lords. In implementing the legislation, doubts have arisen about the ability of authorities to collect the tax with the same level of success as rates were collected. There is evidence, also, that some adults are not registering to vote in order to avoid the tax. All the opposition parties are opposed to the community charge and are pledged to abolish it.

Chapter 7

THE FUTURE OF LOCAL GOVERNMENT

THE previous chapters on local government history, functions and finance have touched on various features of central government control. How these controls have developed is, in many ways, a contemporary history of local government. Since it is central government that chooses when to introduce new legislative controls and how to implement them it is necessary to look at the aims and objectives of the government to try to discern the future role of local government.

It is essential to remember the way in which local government is empowered to act in order to appreciate the full extent to which the government could go if it was determined to make major changes.

Local authorities derive their powers, duties and responsibilities from *Acts of Parliament*. The important principle of *ultra vires*, strictly applied, means that local authorities can only undertake activities which are specially approved by Parliament. These Acts, nevertheless, allow for considerable variation in discretion left with the local authorities.

Statutory powers enacted for local authorities vary widely in terms of discretion. At one end of the spectrum local authorities have no room for local variation. Such items as electoral registration, community charge registration or the unified housing benefit leave little or no power of discretion to the local authorities. The regulations must be carried out to the last detail. However at the other end of the spectrum local authorities can be given general powers to deal with, for example, libraries or swimming baths in whatever way they think necessary.

In essence, therefore, local authority legislation confers powers rather than duties. It was for this reason that it was possible for local authorities to challenge the right of central government to control. If a central government department could not point to statutory provisions authorising intervention then it could not intervene, although it could use other means of persuasion like reduction of grant or delay of approval.

The 1980s

Government policy and consequent legislation in the last few years, however, has tended to turn powers into duties. This means that where an authority had discretionary powers to do, or not do, something, new legislation has defined specifically that an authority must do, or must not do, something. Examples of this trend are instructive. Whereas, in the past, local authorities had power to decide whether contracts for a particular service could be given internally or given to outside contractors they are now, by legislation, obliged to offer the contract to any bidder. Irrespective of the rights and wrongs of this system the fact of the matter is that local discretion has given way to obligation.

Another example of this trend is in housing. In the past local authorities were always free to sell council houses. Now they are obliged to do this if the tenant so wishes. But the tenant's wish is determined by the large discount allowed. That discount is determined by central government and not by the local authority. Legislation currently before Parliament will also allow schools to opt out of the local authority education system. That right can be exercised without reference to the obligation of the education authority to try to cater for the educational needs of the area which they represent and irrespective of the public money put into that school in the past. Once again the authority's discretion has been eroded and replaced by an obligation to do something which central government wishes. One final example is the legislation which allows the Secretary of State for Scotland to determine the level of non-domestic rates, thus replacing the right of the local authority to determine this.

The above remarks illustrate the relationship now between central and local government. In the past that was a working relationship where the central government allowed local authorities to run their area according to the mandate they received from the local electorate, and so long as it conformed to certain national guidelines which ensured that standards would not fall below a certain national minimum. Now the situation is that local authorities appear to be the administrative arm of central government and the veneer of local elections is precisely that, a veneer, an illusion that there is "local democracy". This situation also erodes the right of the local electorate to exercise its political right to choose, or throw out, the local administration.

The Continuing Trend

Statements by leading Conservative politicians suggest that present policies with regard to local government are likely to continue. This means that local authorities will, increasingly, lose local discretionary powers and, also, more sectors of local government services will be put out to tender. We can discern the consequences of this for Scottish local authorities by examining the results of legislation already in existence in England and Wales.

First, in order for the private sector to win council contracts it will have to reduce costs from present levels. In most service areas this usually means reducing wages and conditions since many areas of council services are "labour intensive" and it is difficult to reduce costs by the introduction of modern technology.

Secondly, should a local authority's own "in-house" bid lose to the private sector, it is most unlikely to be able to win back the contract because of loss of experienced staff, non-replacement of equipment, etc. This means that councils will only be able to choose between different levels of service offered by the private companies and not be able to offer a level of service which they deem necessary for their area. Choosing a better standard of service will probably mean increasing the community charge and they will have to assess the likely political consequences of that course of action.

Thirdly, there are many areas of local government services which would be unattractive to the private sector, for example, run-down council housing estates, old people's homes, recreational facilities built in the nineteenth century, etc. These areas of service would probably remain the council's responsibility unless central government were to give a subsidy to the private sector to take them on. If they do remain in the council's hands it will become increasingly difficult for local authorities to find the necessary financial resources for their continuance without, again, central government subvention, failing which, an increase in the community charge.

If the above trends are continued with their resultant scenarios then local authorities, in the future, will probably only meet a few times a year to open batches of tenders for council services or parts of services. This would be nearer to the American local government system where large cities are run by a handful of councilmen who are subjected to all manner of lobbying by a variety of private interest groups and companies wishing to win council contracts. One result of this could be to cast doubt on the probity of councillors and officials, with the consequent demoralisation of staff and elected members who will have to bear the burden of a few who may have corrupted themselves.

The above disturbing picture could make it difficult for councils in the future to recruit able councillors and well-trained and qualified staff. Already some surprising resignations, particularly amongst leading councillors, have been announced for the regional elections of 1990, and the frustration at being unable to influence policy is undoubtedly behind such decisions.

In addition there almost certainly will be a drain away of experienced council staff to the private sector. Indeed this trend has already been established by senior officials in some housing departments taking up posts and directorships in housing associations. This situation could make it difficult to recruit able officials when the private sector can pay more. The local authorities could then see themselves in the position of training officials and then losing them to the private sector. There are, however, wider aspects of the political system which could affect the nature of Scottish local government in the last decade of the twentieth century.

The Future
Local government could develop in several directions. First, there could be the option of continuing to dismember the powers of local authorities, making it harder for them to respond to local needs and aspirations. Secondly, a change in policy from central government could lead to local authorities being granted increased powers and freedoms, although this is very unlikely under a Conservative government which sees predominantly Labour Scottish local authorities as being a threat to their greater aim of reforming Britain as a whole. A third option is that of a constitutional crisis developing in the wake of increased discontent at the ability of an anti-Conservative majority in Scotland being unable to make social policy which reflects its views. Recent election results suggest that just such a discontent is already developing.

It is felt that there needs to be a redefinition of the relationship between central and local power and also between the individual and central government. Now it may be argued that reduction or abolition of local government is a good thing but, in the past, it has always stood as a counterweight to the power of central government. Take local government away and what stands between the individual and centralised government?

One solution may well be that the individual's rights ought to be encompassed in a Bill of Rights as in the American Constitution, but this would require a written constitution, something which the politicians have always argued against but may be forced to think about in the future, especially as the United Kingdom becomes more closely involved in Europe where written constitutions are prevalent.

Another aspect of the present nature and future role of local government is the proposals, widely canvassed amongst Conservatives, that the regional authorities are too big and cumbersome. It is argued that now that many local authority functions have been hived off or privatised, and especially if schools are to be allowed to opt out, there is no need for such big local authorities.

The irony of this approach to the future of local government is the declared policy of all the other parties in Scotland for devolution. (Recent statements from the SNP, however, suggest that it is opposed to devolution, favouring only independence). Should the Conservatives lose power at Westminster then it is almost certain that there will be some sort of Scottish Assembly in Edinburgh. The Labour Party in Scotland already recognises that should there be such a Scottish Assembly there would need to be a consequent reform of local government. Labour Party policy, recently established, points to its recognition of the consequences of devolution on local government. Its solution to this is a proposal to re-establish single-tier local government, albeit with larger units than those which the Conservatives have been thinking about.

Given that the two main parties are approaching much the same conclusion, although from different standpoints, it is almost inevitable that there will be another major reform of local government in the 1990s with the likelihood that the regions will be abolished. Whatever the outcome it seems that local authorities will lose power either to central government or to a Scottish Assembly. The casualty in all this will be local democracy—the power of local people to make local decisions in accordance with local circumstances.

CURRENT FUNCTIONS OF REGIONS AND ISLANDS

Education
    Schools
    Further education colleges
    Community education
    Careers service
    School health service

Social Work
    Children in care
    Physically and mentally handicapped
    Welfare rights
    The elderly

Planning
    Strategic planning
    Industrial development (1)
    Industrial promotion

Protective Services
    Police (2)
    Fire
    Civil defence
    Emergency planning

Transport
    Roads and road safety
    Highways lighting
    Parking
    Urban transportation (2)

Water and Sewerage

Flood Prevention

Coast Protection

Airports, Ferries and Harbours

Miscellaneous
    Consumer protection
    Weights and measures
    Diseases of animals
    Valuation and rating
    Electoral and community charge registration
    Registration of births, marriages and deaths

Notes
(1) Concurrently with districts
(2) No operational control

CURRENT FUNCTIONS OF DISTRICTS

Housing
Council housing
Housing rehabilitation
Housing benefits
Estate management

Planning (1)
Local plans
Development control
Urban redevelopment
Listed buildings and ancient monuments
Conservation areas
Industrial development (concurrently with regions)

Recreation
Libraries (1)
Museums and art galleries
Parks and swimming pools
Nature conservation
Countryside (2)

Environmental Health
Cleansing
Refuse collection and disposal
Public conveniences
Shop hours
Food hygiene
Health and safety at work
Burial and cremation
Markets and slaughterhouses

Miscellaneous
Administration of district courts
Licensing
Community centres (3)
Caravan sites
War memorials
Tourism and publicity

Notes
(1) Except in Borders, Dumfries and Galloway, and Highland where the function is Regional.
(2) Regions have a prescribed role in the countryside also.
(3) Regions can also provide community centres, usually attached to schools.

BIBLIOGRAPHICAL NOTE

Books
There is now a considerable number of general and specific books about local government. Until recently very little of that applied to Scotland, but the continued controversy between central and local government throughout the 1980s has given rise to an increasing number of books and articles. The undernoted books have been found most useful by the authors. For more detailed articles reference should be made to the "recent publications" section of *The Scottish Government Yearbook* which is published annually.

George S. Pryde, *Central and Local Government in Scotland since 1707* (1960).

J. G. Kellas, *The Scottish Political System* (1988).

T. Byrne, *Local Government in Britain* (1981).

M. Keating and A. Midwinter, *The Government of Scotland* (1983).

Keith Ferguson, *An Introduction to Local Government in Scotland* (1984).

Richard Parry, *Scottish Political Facts* (1988).

Official Reports, etc.
As with books there has been a great number of government and other reports. To keep this list manageable and up to date the authors have omitted those which were regarded as important in the first edition but now seem dated or irrelevant to Scotland.

Report of the Royal Commission on Local Government in Scotland (Wheatley), Cmnd. 4150 (1969).

White paper: *Reform of Local Government in Scotland*, Cmnd. 4583 (1971).

Green Paper: *The Future Shape of Local Government Finance*, Cmnd. 4741 (1971).

The New Scottish Local Authorities—Management and Structures (Paterson) (1973).

Housing and Social Work, a joint approach (Morris) (1975).

Report of the Committee of Inquiry into Local Government Finance (Layfield), Cmnd. 6524 (1976).

Scottish Schools Councils: Policy-making, Participation or Irrelevance? (Scottish Education Department) (1980).

Report of the Committee of Inquiry into Local Government in Scotland (Stodart), Cmnd. 8115 (1981).

Alternatives to Domestic Rates, Cmnd. 8449 (1981).

Valuation and Rating in Scotland: Proposals for Reform, Cmnd. 9018 (1983).

Report of the Committee of Inquiry into Functions and Powers of the Island Councils of Scotland (Montgomery), Cmnd. 9216 (1984).

Reports of the Committee of Inquiry into the Conduct of Local Authority Business (Widdicombe), Cmnd. 9797 (1986).

Paying for Local Government, Cmnd. 9714 (1986).

Scottish Homes, a new agency for housing in Scotland (Scottish Development Department) (1987).

School Management: The Government's Conclusions (Scottish Office) (1988).

Other Sources

There are many other sources of information for those dealing with local government in Scotland. The annual reports of the Commission for Local Authority Accounts in Scotland, the Commissioner for Local Authority Administration, and the Chartered Institute of Public Finance and Accountancy (Scottish Branch) make interesting reading about the details of local authority administration. Information can also be obtained from the Convention of Scottish Local Authorities, the Scottish Local Government Information Unit and the Unit for the Study of Government in Scotland (Edinburgh University).

INDEX

Accounts,
    departmental, 59
    housing, 56–58
Accounts Commission. *See* Commission
    for Local Authority Accounts in
    Scotland.
Acts of Parliament,
    Abolition of Domestic Rates Etc.
      (Scotland) 1987, 67, 69
    Employment Protection 1975, 1978,
      35
    generally, 71
    Housing (Homeless Persons) 1977,
      21
    Housing (Scotland) 1987, 21, 28
    Housing (Scotland) 1988, 21–22, 28
    Local Government (Access to Infor-
      mation) 1985, 38
    Local Government 1986, 34
    Local Government 1988, 24, 28, 53,
      61
    Local Government (Scotland) 1929,
      1, 3
    Local Government (Scotland) 1947,
      5
    Local Government (Scotland) 1973,
      1, 7, 34, 48, 60
    Local Government (Scotland) 1975,
      52
    Local Government and Planning
      (Scotland) 1982, 8, 34
    Representation of the People 1983,
      31, 35
    Social Work (Scotland) 1968, 13
    School Boards (Scotland) 1988, 10,
      49
    Town and Country Planning (gener-
      ally), 15
advisory committees, 41
Assisted Places Scheme, 12
attendance allowance, 34, 35
audit,
    external, 60, 61
    internal, 60

Bills,
    Local Government and Housing, 29,
      45
    Self Governing Schools Etc. (Scot-
      land), 10
    Water, 18

boards,
    parochial, 2
    river purification, 18
    school (1872 Act), 3
    school (1988 Act), 49–50
    supply, of, 3
    water, 18
budget, 38, 58–59
burgh system, 1–4

Calling in, 25
candidates, 31–32
capital spending, 56
cash limits, 59
change of use, 26
chief executive, 43
Commission for Local Authority
    Accounts in Scotland, 33–34, 61
Commission for Local Authority
    Administration, 52–54
community charge, 67, 68–70
community councils, 46–48
community education, 12
compulsory competitive tendering,
    28–29
concurrent functions, 14
Controller of Audit, 61
Convention of Scottish Local Authori-
    ties (COSLA), 26–27
co-option, 41, 44, 45
corporate management, 42–43
council(s),
    budget, 38, 58–59
    committees of, 39–42, 42–43
    community, 46–48
    counties of cities, 3
    district, 18–26, Appendix B
    financial year, 58–59
    islands, 26, Appendix A
    meetings, 36–37
    members of, 32–35
    minutes of meetings, 38–39
    municipal year, 38
    officials of, 37
    parish, 3
    political parties, and, 37–38
    powers of, 36–37
    public, and, 38–39
    regional, 9–18, Appendix A
    school, 48–49
council house sales, 19, 57